COMMUNICATE NOW!

A READY RESOURCE FOR TODAY'S ONLINE LEARNER

DR. ARNAB CHATTERJEE

Made with ❤ on the Notion Press Platform
www.notionpress.com

To the learners

Contents

Foreword

In today's rapidly evolving digital landscape, effective communication has become more critical than ever, particularly for online learners. Whether you are a student navigating a virtual classroom or a professional enhancing your skills remotely, the ability to communicate clearly and confidently across digital platforms is essential for success. *Communicate Now! A Ready Resource for Today's Online Learner* addresses this need with practical advice, actionable strategies, and insightful tips to help learners thrive in an online environment.

The internet has revolutionized how we learn, work, and connect with others. As traditional classroom settings continue to shift toward virtual spaces, the need for effective communication skills has never been more urgent. In an online environment, communication isn't just about sharing information; it's about building relationships, fostering collaboration, and ensuring that ideas are expressed and understood with clarity. This book equips readers with the tools they need to excel in this complex landscape.

Communicate Now! takes a comprehensive approach, focusing on both the technical and interpersonal aspects of communication. It covers essential topics such as mastering digital communication tools, engaging in meaningful discussions, navigating group projects, and maintaining professionalism in an online setting. Whether it's a video conference, a forum post, or an email exchange, the strategies provided within these pages will help readers communicate with confidence, empathy, and precision.

One of the standout features of this book is its focus on the unique challenges faced by online learners. The distance between students and instructors, as well as the often impersonal nature of digital platforms, can sometimes lead to misunderstandings and a sense of isolation. *Communicate Now!* addresses these challenges by offering practical advice on how to connect with peers and instructors, overcome communication barriers, and build a sense of community in the virtual space.

Moreover, the book goes beyond the basics of written and spoken communication to include guidance on the nuances of tone, body language (even in virtual settings), and the importance of active listening. These subtle yet powerful skills can make a world of difference in how messages are received and understood.

In the pages that follow, you will find a clear, easy-to-follow roadmap for becoming a more effective communicator in the online world. Whether you are a student new to online learning or someone who has already spent time in virtual classrooms, this book offers practical resources that will empower you to succeed and engage with others more effectively.

Communicate Now! is not just for students—it is a resource for anyone looking to enhance their digital communication skills in a fast-paced, ever-changing world. It is an indispensable guide that will enable you to take charge of your learning experience and emerge as a confident, capable communicator in any online environment. So, take a deep breath, dive in, and get ready to master the art of communication in the digital age from a writer who has a profound knowledge of the ODL system of instruction.

---Dr. Debabrata Hazra
Cambridge Linguaskills Expert
Kommuri Pratap Reddy Institute of Technology
(A UGC declared autonomous institution under JNTU)
Hyderabad.

Preface

Communicate Now! A Ready Resource for Today's Online Learner has been in making for quite some time now. It draws upon my experience both as an online learner as well as an instructor and how today's student, especially within an online setting has to navigate with both job requirements as well as the demands of online and distance education. Moreover, I also work and rework on the hitherto unpublished materials that I previosly prepared as an online instructor and present them for the very first time in a proper book form. As per a report by DEB or the Distance Education Bureau, New Delhi, around twenty five of public instruction in India is accpmplished by this mode, which speaks about the sheer number of online learners who are enrolled in various programmes. Moreover, with the proliferation of MOOCs, especially online platforms like *SWAYAM* and the greater mission of the Government of India like "Digital India", online and distance education is within everyone's reach. The need of the hour is a skilled professional with a sound application base, not just a learner with the smattering of some bare facts and figures.

And yet, to avoid being too erudite, I have not included much of raw data or jargon in the book, so that the greater aim of catering to the online learner who is grappling with the tough requirements of home, job and an online degree does not run into dust. Becoming proficient in a target language like English requires the deft honing of all the four skills, viz., listening, speaking, reading and writing. This means that any "ready resource" should look into the ways in which it can give practical tips, suggestions and snapshots of the topics in an easily assimilable form. Comprehending English as a language is a vast and painful exercise, and without the learner face to face in a class, this becomes an even more utopian a dream. Thus, any resource or even a handbook must come down to the level of the learner and put the matter in plain terms. I have tried to accomplish so. My readers are the best judge now and I leave it to them. Charts and pictures have been taken from Creative Commons.

I am thankful to Notion Press, Chennai for the stupendous DIY platform that is well catering to the writers who can see their books now in print, with the rude fact that most of the publishing houses today are already clogged with submissions waiting in the "pipeline". Thanks are also due to the Centre for Distance and Online Education, Chandigarh University for inspiring me to work on a project like this, with more on the way. I also dedicate this book to my daughter Celina, my wife Rinki and my pet dog Bruno for their unconditional love. Lastly, a heart-felt thanks to my learned colleagues and superiors alike in the said centre for inspiring me to move forward. And my salutations to my departed parents, Late Sri Bhaskar Chatterjee and Late Smt. Rupa Chatterjee who give me peace in troubled times. This book is also for them who were my first teachers at school.

---Dr. Arnab Chatterjee
Chandigarh
India.
February 2025.
Mobile: +91-9330473173
Email: carnab393@gmail.com

CHAPTER ONE

Introduction

Communicate Now! A Ready Resource for the Online Learner draws upon my experience both as an online and distance education teacher as well as a learner, along with my own attempts to grapple with the work-study binary coupled with the question of technology as well as pedagogy within this conceptual matrix. Online and distance education has been in vogue for a very long time, despite the relatively new attempts to integrate the teacher as well as the learner via synchronous and asynchronous modes. Perhaps the earliest of attempts was in 1728, when it was advertised in the *Boston Gazette* regarding a teacher "Caleb Philipps", who sought to teach short hand through weekly mailed materials. However, the first distance education course in the modern sense of the term was started by Sir Issac Pitman in the 1840s, who sought to teach short hand again through transcriptions on postcards, and asking a return for corrections. Finally, the University of London in 1858 established its "External Programme" to anyone who could pass their examinations.

While educationists as well as liberal thinkers see the ODL mode as a kind of 'democratization' of the education system, so that it is freely accessible for all, it nevertheless comes with its own unique set of challenges. John M. Keller (b. 1986), the renowned educational psychologist came up with his ARCS Model in 1979. His work was in the domain of instructional design and how external stimuli has to be shifted to learner's motivational systems that was a shift from the previous cognitive and behaviourist practices. His model that stressed Attention, Relevance, Confidence and Satisfaction as the key metrics that can address the success of the teaching-learning mechanism. The model was also well-attuned with his doctoral work on instructional technology at Indiana University, Bloomington in 1974. It looks Keller was, in one way, responding to the significant drop-out rates and discontinuation of courses in ODL modes, and this might have enabled him to work in the arena of instructional design and pedagogy that puts the learner firmly within the "conceptual grid" of the ARCS Model. The big question that still faces an online and even distance education learner is—why a course should be pursued and how to circumvent the economic as well as technological constraints? Though there has been a huge proliferation of MOOCs and the e-learning portals as well as teacher training programmes both in India and abroad, ODL modes still suffer from the way teaching-learning has to be made more 'interesting' and 'relevant', thus catapulting back to Keller's Model. The study in 2011 on the Washington State Community College students shows how students drop out from such a mode of education owing to issues with "language, time management and study skills." Moreover, putting and assessing online and traditional programmes on the same pedestal is a grave error as it ignores the efforts of the online teacher as an active generator of a unique instructional discourse within a non-traditional setting.

Furthermore, distance learning mechanisms are often enhanced by multimedia tools, such as interactive video lessons, podcasts, and discussion forums. These tools offer a rich and varied learning experience that goes beyond traditional textbooks. For example, listening to native speakers in real-life contexts, participating in online conversations, and using language apps for pronunciation practice can significantly improve speaking and listening skills. These multimedia resources also help learners immerse themselves in the language, simulating real-world communication scenarios.

Another significant benefit of ODL is the access to global communities and support networks. Online platforms allow learners to connect with others from different parts of the world, providing an opportunity for cross-cultural communication. This exposure to different accents, idioms, and dialects further enhances the learner's ability to adapt and understand diverse English communication styles. Additionally, many distance learning courses offer interaction with instructors and fellow students through chat rooms, video calls, or social media, creating a sense of community and fostering peer learning.

However, the success of ODL in teaching English communication depends on the learner's motivation and discipline. Without the structure of a traditional classroom, learners must take initiative and manage their time effectively. For some, the lack of direct supervision can be a challenge, requiring strong self-regulation and consistency.

Open and Distance Learning mechanisms offer a wide array of benefits for those learning to communicate in English. The flexibility, multimedia tools, and global learning opportunities make ODL an effective and accessible option for improving language skills. However, for learners to succeed, they must remain motivated and disciplined in their approach to learning. With the right attitude and the support of these innovative learning tools, mastering English communication is within reach for many. And yet, despite the best of efforts, the learner is at odds to gain proficiency in the target language like English, especially when it comes to teaching it in the traditional classroom, let alone in an ODL setting. This means that teaching a subject like Communicative English within a synchronous as well as asynchronous setup is a major challenge, especially when it comes to inculcating all the four skills, viz., LSRW in the learner. While one can use all the tools available under the 4Q or quadrant approach, sceptics would be quick to point out that no foreign language can be taught in this way. Of course, we have a host of online language learning platforms like *Duolingo*, *Cambly*, etc. that employ native English speakers. Theodore Osagie Iyere in his article "Teaching Spoken English in the ODL System in Nigeria; Challenges and Strategies for Improvement" (2010) talks about the topic in some detail vis-à-vis using the ODL mode for teaching a target language, a known mode of communication in the African nation. Many Open and Distance Education institutes and other HEIs have a course on the *Pedagogy of Teaching English* that talks about the nuances of teaching the subject in both traditional as well as non-traditional modes. Cambridge English discusses along numerous verticals like "remote teaching guides", "free teaching resources", "online teaching webinars" and a host of techniques to ensure quality control. CIQA or Centre for Internal Quality Assurance is an internal body within an ODL setup that monitors lesson delivery, video quality and other associated parameters. Though mountains of data exist on the pedagogy of teaching in an ODL matrix, it now becomes germane on my part to explain how the book functions within this scenario of communicative competence for an L2 like English.

Firstly, it is pertinent on my part to present a general overview of grammar. Though much debate exists on the use and 'abuse' of grammar in meaningful contexts, there is no denying the fact that the proper use of basic structures of grammar is needed for communicative competence. Thus, this document presents a general overview of grammar within the ODL setup. Since any resource on grammar can get tedious, breaking the entire document into microunits enables the author to aim at what we christen "micro-learning"—how students can benefit from around 15-20 minutes of reading material without fatigue. Secondly, it is also an aim to use examples in meaningful, communicative contexts that a learner can relate to one's surroundings and the corresponding linguistic environment. Today's online student comes from many different scenarios, ranging from a student to a high-paced professional. As the time is less, even though the learner can study at one's own pace, serving a student a huge chunk of material can be unnerving. This means that the teacher-counsellor has to dole such materials as micro-units that can be easily assimilated by the learner. Secondly, it has to be kept in mind that the ready resource looks forward to building the confidence of the student and thus, materials have been divided and sub-divided thematically. This is expected to facilitate easy comprehension and assimilation. At times, exercises have been also provided that test the progression of the students, as this is of paramount importance in an online setting.

I hope the *Ready Resource* will be beneficial to today's online learner who is busy straddling the difficult binary of being a deft professional and a learner at the same time.

CHAPTER TWO

Grammar Again! Now What?

It looks you don't like grammar. Well, you know what? Even I don't!

Who would care if a noun cannot be a verb or even a preposition? Afterall, we don't think of grammar when we communicate. If we do,that would make us stammer or even shy away from a real conversation. Right? No one in his or her right senses would take a dusty book of Nesfield or Wren and Martin to get along with the difference between a participle and a gerund. You have the biggest invention of the 21st century: Google. Type and you're there. Or, if too many search results get on your nerves, try any open source AI. But experts believe that a minimum, working knowledge of grammar is indeed needed for communicative competence. Grammar plays a crucial role in communication as it provides structure and clarity to language. This ensures that ideas are conveyed accurately and effectively, preventing misunderstandings. It helps readers or listeners follow the intended message, making it easier to engage with the content. Without correct grammar, sentences can become confusing or ambiguous, which can distort meaning and hinder the flow of communication. In both written and spoken forms, using grammar correctly enhances credibility and professionalism, allowing individuals to express themselves more persuasively and with greater impact.

Grammar plays a crucial role in effective communication, acting as the framework that helps convey meaning clearly and precisely. Whether spoken or written, grammar ensures that messages are structured in a way that listeners or readers can easily interpret. Without proper grammar, language can become muddled, leading to confusion, misunderstanding, and sometimes even the failure of communication. The importance of grammar can be observed in various aspects of life, including education, professional settings, personal relationships, and more.

One of the primary reasons grammar is so important in communication is that it ensures clarity. Grammar rules govern the structure of sentences—how words are ordered, what tenses are used, and how different parts of speech are combined. For instance, the difference between "Let's eat, grandma" and "Let's eat grandma" illustrates how punctuation and grammar can completely change the meaning of a sentence. Proper grammar removes ambiguity and allows the message to be conveyed with precision.

In written communication, clarity is especially crucial. When sending an email, writing a report, or composing any professional document, the ability to articulate ideas clearly can influence the outcome. A well-structured, grammatically correct piece of writing conveys the sender's competence and helps avoid misunderstandings.

In professional settings, grammar serves as a tool for creating a positive image. The way individuals write or speak reflects their level of education, attention to detail, and respect for their audience. Poor grammar, on the other hand, can suggest carelessness, lack of education, or even a lack of respect for the listener or reader. This can lead to negative perceptions, especially in contexts where professionalism is highly valued.

For instance, a cover letter or resume with numerous grammatical errors may reduce the chances of landing a job, as employers could perceive the candidate as unprofessional or careless. Similarly, in business communication, whether through emails or presentations, incorrect grammar can undermine the credibility of the speaker and the message they are trying to convey.

Grammar also plays a significant role in promoting understanding between individuals. Communication often involves multiple parties, each with their own perspective, background, and language proficiency. By adhering to standard grammatical rules, communicators increase the likelihood that their message will be understood as intended. For example, using consistent verb tenses allows listeners or readers to follow the timeline of events easily. Proper punctuation helps distinguish between statements, questions, and exclamations, ensuring that the tone and intent of the message are correctly interpreted.

In multilingual environments, where people may not share the same native language, standard grammar becomes even more essential. When speakers use correct grammar, it can help bridge the gap between diverse language speakers and ensure smoother, more efficient communication.

In education, grammar is essential for both teaching and learning. For students, learning grammar provides the foundation for acquiring a language. It is only through understanding the rules that students can express themselves with accuracy. In language education, grammar instruction helps students construct sentences properly and communicate in a way that makes sense to others.

On the other hand, teachers rely on grammar to convey lessons in a structured manner. Teachers also use grammar to evaluate students' language proficiency. In written essays or oral presentations, grammatical accuracy can be a reflection of a student's understanding of the language. Furthermore, the systematic nature of grammar allows for objective grading in academic settings, where language competency is essential.

Grammar provides a structure that brings consistency to language use. It offers rules that govern sentence construction, word choice, and punctuation, ensuring that language remains organized and predictable. This consistency is particularly important in written texts such as manuals, guides, legal documents, and academic papers. In these contexts, accuracy and consistency are paramount because any inconsistency can lead to confusion or misinterpretation.

For example, in legal language, the precise use of grammar can make the difference between a binding agreement and a vague suggestion. The phrase "The party may terminate the contract at any time" has a very different implication than "The party shall terminate the contract at any time." The first sentence offers an option, while the second imposes an obligation. Without grammar, such distinctions would be lost, undermining the effectiveness of the communication.

The way we use grammar also influences how persuasive and impactful our communication is. In both public speaking and written persuasion, clarity, tone, and structure matter greatly. A well-constructed argument, supported by correct grammar, appears more credible and compelling. On the contrary, a persuasive speech or essay that lacks proper grammar can come across as less authoritative and more difficult to follow.

Consider political speeches, advertisements, or marketing campaigns. The success of these forms of communication depends not only on the content but also on how the language is structured. Grammar affects the emotional appeal (pathos), the logical structure (logos), and the trustworthiness (ethos) of the message. A message that is grammatically sound is more likely to resonate with the audience and elicit the desired response.

Grammar is also instrumental in preserving the integrity of languages and cultures. Each language has its own set of grammatical rules, which helps maintain its unique characteristics. The study of grammar allows individuals to understand the history and evolution of their language. It also enables people to pass down traditions, stories, and customs that are embedded in language. Without grammar, languages could devolve into incoherent fragments, losing their richness and the cultural significance tied to them.

Furthermore, grammar plays a vital role in translation. Translating ideas from one language to another involves not just converting words but also accurately capturing grammatical structures. Effective grammar is needed to maintain the integrity of the original message while adapting it for the target audience. This ensures that the meaning of the communication is preserved.

In complex or specialized fields, such as law, science, and medicine, the importance of grammar cannot be overstated. These fields often require highly precise communication to avoid errors that could have significant consequences. In these contexts, even a small grammatical mistake can alter the meaning of a statement, leading to confusion or dangerous misinterpretation.

For instance, in medical prescriptions, a misplaced comma could change the dosage of a medication, potentially causing harm. Similarly, in scientific research papers, proper grammar ensures that complex theories are communicated with accuracy, allowing other researchers to build upon them without misunderstanding the original concepts.

It is still a matter of heated debate if a real understanding of grammar and its rules is needed for communicative competence in the target language, especially English. The Dutch linguist Simon Dik (1940-1995) believed in the functional aspects of language use than mere insistence on the memorisation of bland rules of grammar. University of Cambridge's Assessment exam, called the BEC or Business English Certification syllabus and materials seem to emphasise the use of grammar in meaningful, functional contexts of business environments. Although various levels of grammar have been identified by Avram Noam Chomsky, the American linguist (1928-) and even though the British linguist M.A.K. Halliday (1925-2018) insisted on the "systemic functional" aspects of grammar that sees the overall language system as a repository of meaning within social contexts, the feasibility of teaching grammar in classrooms and with what methodology still needs to be decided. With the advent of communicative language teaching (CLT) that is firmly situated within the conceptual matrix of need-based learning and communication as the end of classroom practices, grammar is likely to be relegated to the rear. Still, a real understanding of grammatical rules will nevertheless help the learner speak and write correctly. No amount of fluency can hide palpable errors with recourse to language use and grammar is one of those parameters that both defines as well as regulates meaning.

A working definition

The field of grammar has been variously defined. It is:

a. As per the *Longman Dictionary of Language Teaching & Applied Linguistics* (2010), grammar is "a description of the structure of a language and the way in which linguistic units such as words and phrases are combined to produce sentences in the language. It usually takes into account the meanings and functions these sentences have in the overall system of the language. "It may or may not include the description of the sounds of a language" (p.251-52).

b. Another definition of grammar is that it is the language user's "internal system" of comprehending and ordering language.

c. Grammar may also be defined as that body of rules that lets a s peaker speak, write and order correct language use in a variety of contexts.

d. The *Merriam-Webster* defines it as "the study of the classes of words, their inflections, and their functions and relations in a sentence".

The three levels of grammar

It is noteworthy that the concept of grammar operates at three (3) levels

a. **G1:** The G1 level refers to the total mechanism that a language possesses and through which its users are able to communicate with each other. Any native speaker can control his/her G1.

b. **G2:** The G2 level refers to the formal descriptions and analysis of a language in form of its grammar.

c. **G3:** The G3 level refers to the rules of 'correct' usage that may be prescribed for its users.

Self-Assessment Questions

1. Halliday's approach to language and the grammatical system is known as:

    A. Systemic-Functional
    B. Generative
    C. Both
    D. None

2. The full form of BEC is.

    A. British English Certification
    B. Business English Certification
    C. Benchmark English Certification
    D. Bloom's English Certification

3. Many experts have expressed doubts about the learning of the rules of grammar. The given statement is.

    A. True
    B. False
    C. Cannot be determined from the passage
    D. None

4. Which of the given is not a kind of grammar?

    A. G1
    B. G2
    C. G5
    D. G7

5. Which of the following defines grammar as "a description of the structure of a language and the way in which linguistic units such as words and phrases are combined"?

    A. The Merriam-Webster
    B. Hornby's Dictionary
    C. Advanced Oxford Dictionary of Current English

D. Longman's Dictionary of Language Teaching & Applied Linguistics

A. Nouns: Countable and Uncountable

When we learn about a new noun, we should be aware if we know how to use it whether as a countable or an uncountable noun as per British Council.[1]

Look at some of the nouns given below and analyse them as either countable or uncountable:

Advice, Luggage, Milk, Apples, Oranges, Water

As you can see from these nouns, some of them can be counted while others cannot be. For instance, you can count the number of apples or oranges you have inside your bag or fridge, but you cannot count either "advice" or "water" in that way. While it is true that you can count the number of glasses of water on your table, you cannot 'count' the amount of water in each glass. Similar is the case with "milk" or "advice". With regards to the word "advice" it is fast becoming a trend to use the determiner "a" before the same:

1. I'd like to give you **some** advice [uncountable]
2. I'd like to give you **a** piece of advice. [countable]

The way we use both countable as well as uncountable nouns shows our ability to use this part of grammar correctly that leads to better competence in language use. Another feature of an uncountable noun is that it cannot be made into a plural—thus, the plural of "furniture" is furniture and the plural of "advice" is advice. However, there have been a good number of exceptions; it has been a common feature to use the plural "s" after "water" to make it "waters":

Example: The mermaid disappeared into the cold **waters** of the sea from where she had come.

It is a common practice to use content words in a sentence and the rest of the stuff is basically followed by functional words. Content words are words that usually have a quick and ready dictionary meaning while functional words have to deal with modals, pronouns, prepositions and the like.

1. **A solved exercise for you**

1. The **children** are playing in the garden.
2. I don't like **milk**.
3. I prefer **tea**.
4. **Scientists** say that the environment is threatened by pollution.
5. My mother uses **butter** to prepare cakes.
6. There are a lot of **windows** in our classroom.
7. We need some **glue** to fix this vase.
8. The **waiters** in this restaurant are very professional.
9. My father drinks two big **glasses** of water every morning.
10. The **bread** my mother prepares is delicious.
11. **Drivers** must be careful; the road is slippery.
12. Some **policemen** are organising road traffic to avoid any accidents.
13. I bought three **bottles** of mineral water for our picnic.
14. I'd like some **juice** please.

15. Successful **candidates** will join the camp later this year.
16. A rise in **oil** prices is inevitable since there is more and more world demand for energy.
17. The **exercises** on this website are interesting.
18. Dehydrated babies must drink a lot of **water**.
19. Adult illiterates learn through a special government **program**.

Self-Assessment Questions

6. What is true about uncountable nouns?

    A. They cannot be made into a plural at all
    B. They can be but with exceptions
    C. Neither (i) nor (ii)
    D. The concept of uncountable nouns itself is faulty

7. "All the peoples of this world unite". The given sentence is:

    A. Correct

B. Incorrect

C. Can't say

D. Depends on the context

8. The concept of uncountable nouns is important as:

    A. We use them frequently in our daily conversation
    B. They are particularly important in business settings
    C. They are an important part of the grammatical structure
    D. All

9. "There is a **glass of milk** on the table."--- the words in bold show that the same is:

    A. A countable noun
    B. An uncountable noun
    C. Both countable as well as uncountable
    D. The sentence is confusing and hence cannot be determined.

B. **Tenses**

The three basic structures in a language system's grammar are tense, verb patterns and the use of prepositions. Tense is of cardinal importance as it helps us drive home the point of time —to what extent the agent is situated within a reliable timeframe. For example, read these 4 sentences below:

    ---Venkata has been reading the novel since 2020.

    ---Venkata would have finished the novel by then. **[when?]**

    ---Venkata would have been reading the novel by then.

    ---Venkata is reading the novel right now.

In all the four (4) examples, you can definitely notice a fine slant and play in the meaning of words. While the first example definitely tells us about the timeframe (since 2020), little or no clue is provided as regards the rest sentences. For instance, in sentence no. 2, the information as to "when" would Venkata have finished reading the novel has not been furnished and we are just left guessing. Even the last sentence gives us little clue; we are just sure that Venkata "is" reading the novel "right now".

Grammarians Wren and Martin in their *High School English Grammar & Composition* define verb as "...a word that tells and asserts something about a person or thing. Verb comes from the Latin "verbum", meaning a word. It is so called because it is the most important word in a sentence" (54). [2]

1. **Present and Past**

Simple present and simple past tense denote basic actions that occur in the present and occurred in the past. Simple present denotes an action that happens in the present and should not be confused with present continuous wherein the action continues for a considerable period of time.

2. **Simple Present**

   1. The boy runs
   2. The bell rings
   3. The man eats ten rotis.
   4. I eat and drink

On the contrary, present continuous denotes an action that began at some point in the present but tends to continue for a considerable period of time. It is indicative of the doer who is still engaged in the action and is in the very thick of it:

3. **Present Continuous**

   1. The boy is running.
   2. The bell is ringing.
   3. The man is eating ten rotis.
   4. I am eating and drinking.

4. **Simple Past and Continuous**

Simple past denotes an action that occurred in the past and stopped then and there:

   1. I ate a mango.
   2. I spent the summer vacations in Kashmir.

3. Ravi submitted a job application yesterday.
4. I told the students to bring their laptops to the class.

In each of these sentences, you can easily note that the action began somewhat in the past and does not continue till date or has just happened as in case of simple present. Simple past tense thus denotes an action that began in the past and ended there and is not carried forward.

Simple Past Continuous, at the other end of the spectrum, denotes an action that began in the past but an impression is given that it **continued** in the past for some time. Thus, imagine you bought an ice-cream yesterday and enjoyed it for some time, at least an hour. That memory lingers in you and you've to express the same in words. How you'd you go about it? It is here that a working knowledge of tense, especially past continuous helps you express your memory of the incident. Examples include:

1. I was eating an ice-cream yesterday at the park.
2. Simran and Srinivas were talking in a restaurant the other day.
3. I was going to a weekend party yesterday when you saw me.
4. I was reading a book when you called me on the 12th of this month at 2 PM.

5. Present and Past Perfect

Look at the following sentences

A. He has just eaten a biscuit.

A. He has just tendered his resignation.

B. He had written the email before he joined the institution. He had been to Delhi then when we called him.

In the first two sentences, we have an action that has just been accomplished, while in the next group, it has to do with an action completed before a certain moment in the past. The sentences in group A are written in **present perfect,** while those in B are in **past perfect**. The hallmark of such sentences is that the auxiliary **has, have or had** is added and the past participle form of the verb is used.

Self-Assessment Questions

10. Arrange these sentences written in simple past in the probable order of their occurrence:

0. There was no one in the room
i. I heard a sound in the next room
ii. It was around 3 AM in the morning
iii. I was asleep in my bedroom
iv. I checked the room thoroughly
v. I felt a bit awkward as I live all alone in the flat

    a. i, ii, iii, iv, v, vi
    b. ii, i, iii, iv, v, vi
    c. vi, v, iii, i, vi, ii
    d. iv, ii, iii, v, i, vi

C. Understanding and Interpreting Texts

The word "text" comes from a Latin word "textus" which means to weave. Thus, the concept of weaving multiple viewpoints and narratives is closely aligned with that of a text. But the question is: what is a text?

In plain language and for general understanding, what was previously called a book or even a passage to fall back to during a classroom lecture is now called a "text". This paradigm shift was the result of a famous essay by the French philosopher of language and a semiotician called Roland Barthes (1915-1980) [pronounced "Rola Barth"] whose essay "From Work to Text" (1977) opened up new possibilities in the interpretation of the sign system at work. After this, the text was more fittingly called a discourse — a treatise or a plan of action that may incorporate anything from the book you are reading to the culture that you cherish.

Let us now see the kinds of texts:

1. **Narrative Texts** are texts that narrate incidents and often may contain case studies that, in turn, narrate and describe the entire thing in form of a story or a plot. Narratives contain facts and figures essentially, but they explain the entire stuff in form of a narrative of sorts. Case studies may be narrative or analytical in approach.

2. **Expository Texts** expose facts and information but may contain more complex grammatical structures. Expository texts give information about various issues. For example, a text of 500 words that gives you information about the newly launched iPhone in the market may be considered an expository text.

3. **Informative Texts** are also expository in nature, but the main difference is that while expository texts often seek to persuade the reader within the first paragraph, informative texts may not have that intention. Also, informative texts do not contain personal opinions while expository texts might end up having them as per Pen & the Pad.

4. **Analytical Texts** are texts that often use the tools of analysis and introspection. Suppose you are reading a poem in the class and after it has been finished, your professor tells you to write a critical note about the same. The critical note that you write is an example of an analytical text. The source text (the poem here) is analysed in the light of available evidence and facts.

5. **Didactic Texts** contain a moral. They are sermonising in nature and tend to preach rather than inform or persuade. Even though the Panchatantra tales contain a moral at the end, they are not didactic in the real sense of the term. Examples include the Bhagavada Gita or a sermon by a monk in a monastery.

6. **Argumentative Texts** are marked by their critical stance and persuasive nature, with the first predominating. They may take various forms. For instance, in the famous scene in William Shakespeare's Julius Caesar (1599), Antony's speech that he has come to "bury Caesar, not to praise him" is an excellent example of oratory as it is an argumentative text. Any court proceedings and the arguments put forth by a lawyer to save his/her client is one of the most readily available instances of argumentative texts in daily use.

7. **E-Texts** are digital content that most of us access today. They do not have a physical existence as a book chapter but are rather located in the cloud or might be accessed via a subscription. One of the easiest ways of accessing electronic or e-texts is either through a paid subscription to various blogs

and websites or by accessing them via a Kindle App or a device that offers cloud-based options.

Self-Assessment Questions

11. The *Panchatantra* tales are perfect examples of a didactic text ---the given statement is:

a. True
b. False
c. Both true as well as false
d. They are not didactic but rather e-texts exclusively

12. Which of the following is not true about e-texts?

a. They are stored within a digital environment
b. They are available via a subscription
c. They are accessible via a cloud network
d. They have no authors and anyone can edit them

13. An argument put forward by a lawyer in a court is a perfect example of:

a. An argumentative text
b. An expository text
c. A didactic text
d. None

14. Case studies can be narrative or expository this means:

a. Case studies can be read like a story of sorts
b. Case studies seek to present facts and figures
c. Neither (a) nor (b)
d. Both (a) and (b)

15. Which of the following is used in analytical texts?

a. Critical analysis
b. Introspection
c. Didacticism
d. Argumentation

D. Application of Various Texts in Workplace Situations
i. What is a workplace?

Understanding texts and their applicability in various workplace situations to transact a business is a key life skill. The WHO or World Health Organisation in 1990s identified certain key life skills as per hangoutagile.com and one of them is communicative skills You may well appreciate that communication skills are of paramount importance in today's workplace, as they are in any contextual environment that begets such skills. But then, what exactly is a "workplace"?

A workplace may be defined as a social sphere where like-minded people possessing similar skill sets and aspirations work to achieve a common goal or target. A workplace may often take forms of an office or any space within an organisation that looks forward to achieving a target within a viable timeframe. Any self-employed person might also have a workplace in his/her home or at a convenient location. Closely linked with the concept of a workplace is a "workstation" —the tools and necessary support mechanisms that are needed to carry on the designated task within the workplace. It might consist of things as simple as a pen or a laptop computer to that of a well- defined direction from the management to follow certain set rules and thereby achieve a target.

ii. A sample text

So, how are different kinds of texts we just had a look related to workplace situations? One way of answering the question is to see what these texts do in the workplace and how are we supposed to react to them to maximise output and efficiency. To make matters simple, have a look at the note that a Mr. Richards left for his secretary Lucie as he has an urgent appointment with the CEO of the company in another city and would not be coming down to his office for the rest of the day:

Dear Lucie:

I shall be busy with Mr. Andrews for the rest of the day. You are urged to take special note of the following:

1. Inform the shortlisted clients to be ready for a demo regarding the product the next week.
2. Send the email to DelTex regarding the problem we had the last week with the consignment.
3. Look into the profile of Technotronix Inc., New Jersey.
4. Call Freddy to ask him to list the problems he had of late with Miss Bennet.
5. Give me a call sharp at 5 PM to call home
6. Draft an e-notice and send it to our website developer regarding the Christmas vacations.

Based on your understanding of the various texts that we just saw and their features, what kind of a text do you think this is. Since the one here is just concerned with giving some bare information and instructions, it is an instance of an informative text as the sole idea is to give clear-cut instructions to the secretary Lucie so that she has a fairly good idea of what she has to accomplish even in the absence of her Boss for the rest of the day. Another conspicuous feature of the text here is that it does not contain any personal opinions of the Boss here in question. This sets it aside from either expository texts or even narrative texts that seek to narrate. It cannot be a didactic text either as the aim here is not to drive home a moral but to create a dataset to achieve tangible goals.

Self-Assessment Questions

16.Which of the following is a feature of a workplace?

0. A workstation
a. People
b. Clear directions from top management
c. All

17. In the sample text where Mr. Andrews leaves a message for his secretary Lucie, the tone of the text is:

0. Official
a. Personal
b. Impersonal
c. Both (a) and (b)

18. A workplace is basically a social sphere where like-minded individuals work. This means:

0. It is a social space
a. It is a cultural space
b. It is an economic space
c. All

19. The WHO lists communicative skills as a basic skill. The reason could be:

0. They are vital for correspondence
a. They are vital for the negotiation of meaning
b. They are vital for professional excellence
c. All

20. The number of vital life skills as per WHO is:
(a) 20
(b) 10
(c) 14
d) 19

Summary

Grammar is a study of the various rules of a language system that lets a person negotiate meaning and thereby achieve proficiency in the target language in a variety of contexts. Grammar may also be seen as that aspect of a language system that helps understand the structure of the language as far as correct use of those structures is concerned.

Nouns may be classified as both countable as well as uncountable. Countable nouns are those structures that can be numerically classified, whereas in case of uncountable nouns, they cannot be.

Tenses are three in number: Present, Past and Future. Present tense is used for incidents that occur in the immediate present. Past tense concerns itself with incidents of the past and future tense with events concerning incidents slated to happen in future.

The word "text" comes from the Latin epithet "textus" which means to weave. This reinforces the idea of multiple viewpoints or discourses being incorporated in the same text. Texts can be of many types, but the primary ones include didactic texts, informative texts, expository texts, argumentative texts and E-texts.

Understanding texts and their nature and the purpose that they serve is of cardinal importance and is a skill that helps one excel in the workplace. In the example that we saw the directions left by the Boss to his secretary to execute certain tasks depends on the ability of the latter to understand such instructions in particular contexts within which they occur and with what consequences.

Terminal Questions

1. How would you define grammar? Why do you think a working knowledge of grammar is of paramount importance along with one's ability to speak fluently?

2. "Understanding the kinds of texts and their function in day-to-day life is of cardinal importance". Do you agree with this view? Why or why not?

3. What function do you feel tense plays in the correct negotiation of meaning? Answer with reference to any two such functions.

Activity

Type: Offline Duration: 40 minutes

Description

Stephen is a first year Master's student at the XYZ Institute of Technology, New Delhi. He is proud of his spoken English skills and, to that end, ends up sporting a superiority complex. But he commits visible mistakes in grammar while speaking. However, after the end of the first year, the first phase campus recruitment drive was conducted and he was interviewed by a logistics company based in Bangalore. During the interview, he was assessed based on his communicative skills. He was asked his personal opinions through certain open- ended questions, his hobbies and his plans for the future. He answered all of them with gusto and enthusiasm but when the results of the campus drive came, he scored a dismal C+ when the minimum criterion was at least a B.

Now answer the questions

a. Why do you think Stepehen fared badly in the campus drive? Do you think it has to do something with his weakness in grammar?
b. From this brief case study, do you think that learning grammar is of paramount importance?
c. Do communicative skills incorporate both communicative competence as well as grammatical competence? What do you think?

End Notes

1. British Council. *Learn English.* https://www.learnenglish.britishcouncil.org. Accessed 10 March 2024.

2. P.C. Wren & H. Martin. (2007) *High School English Grammar & Composition.* Rev. by
N D V Prasada Rao. New Delhi: Sultan Chand.

SHORT BIBLIOGRAPHY

External Resources

Bennie, M. (2009) *A Guide to Good Business Communication.* How to Books. 5th ed.

Lewis, N. (2019) *30 Days to Better English.* Penguin.

Wren, P. C., & Martin, H. (2007) *High School English Grammar & Composition.* Rev. by N D V Prasada Rao. New Delhi: S Chand.

Video Links

Nouns: Countable and Uncountable
https://www.youtube.com/watch?v=1LjTa2Wvmm0
Tense
https://www.youtube.com/watch?v=69lzkfvFUqQ
Workplace Communication
https://www.youtube.com/watch?v=knUEdy-kOIQ
Types of Texts
https://www.youtube.com/watch?v=9-NECk2aYxU
Keywords
Countable

Uncountable
Textus
Discourse
Business communication

CHAPTER THREE

The Building Blocks

The structural system of the English language is an intricate network of rules and patterns that govern how words, phrases, and sentences are constructed to convey meaning. Grammar, as a part of the structural system, encompasses these rules and guidelines. Understanding how the English language is structured can enhance communication, improve writing, and help learners master the language. This essay will explore the various components of the English language's structural system, focusing particularly on its grammar. At the foundation of English structure is phonology, which deals with the sounds of the language. Phonology provides the rules for how sounds are produced and combined to form words. English has a complex phonological system, including consonants, vowels, and diphthongs, all of which work together to create spoken language.

Each English word is made up of phonemes—the smallest units of sound that can distinguish one word from another. For example, the words "bat" and "pat" differ by one phoneme, the initial sound /b/ vs. /p/. Phonological rules also govern stress patterns in words and sentences, influencing meaning and pronunciation. For instance, "record" as a noun is stressed on the first syllable ("RE-cord"), but as a verb, it is stressed on the second syllable ("re-CORD").

Though English spelling does not always match pronunciation exactly, phonology is a foundational aspect of how words are formed and spoken.

Morphology is the branch of linguistics that focuses on the internal structure of words. In English, words are typically made up of morphemes—the smallest units of meaning. A morpheme could be a standalone word (e.g., "book"), a prefix (e.g., "un-"), or a suffix (e.g., "-ed"). The structure of morphemes within words is what allows English to create a vast number of words by combining different parts.

There are two main types of morphemes in English: free morphemes and bound morphemes. Free morphemes can stand alone as words (e.g., "cat," "run"), while bound morphemes must attach to other morphemes to convey meaning (e.g., "un-" in "undo" or "-ing" in "running").

Syntax is the set of rules that governs how words are arranged into phrases, clauses, and sentences. The basic word order in English is Subject-Verb-Object (SVO). This means that in a simple sentence, the subject (the "doer" of the action) typically comes first, followed by the verb (the action), and finally the object (the recipient of the action).

For example:

"The cat (S) chased (V) the mouse (O)."

While this basic structure holds for most simple sentences, English syntax becomes more complex when modifiers, clauses, and other elements are added. English allows for a great deal of flexibility in sentence structure, such as the use of questions, negations, and various clauses. For example, in questions, the auxiliary verb often precedes the subject:

"Did you see the movie?"

Similarly, negation is achieved through the addition of the auxiliary verb "not":

"I do not know the answer."

The placement of adjectives and adverbs in English also follows specific syntactical rules. Adjectives generally precede the noun they modify:

"The big house"

Adverbs often appear after the verb or at the end of the sentence:

"She sings beautifully."

The structure of English grammar also relies on understanding the different parts of speech. These categories organize words according to their function in a sentence. The primary parts of speech in English include:

Nouns: Represent people, places, things, or ideas (e.g., "dog," "city," "happiness").

Verbs: Express actions, states, or occurrences (e.g., "run," "is," "seem").

Adjectives: Modify or describe nouns (e.g., "big," "happy," "blue").

Adverbs: Modify or describe verbs, adjectives, or other adverbs (e.g., "quickly," "very," "here").

Pronouns: Replace nouns to avoid repetition (e.g., "he," "it," "they").

Prepositions: Show relationships between other words in a sentence, often indicating direction, time, or place (e.g., "in," "on," "before").

Conjunctions: Connect words, phrases, or clauses (e.g., "and," "but," "or").

Interjections: Express strong feelings or reactions (e.g., "wow," "ouch," "hey").

These parts of speech play a crucial role in determining how a sentence is constructed and understood, and they interact according to the syntactic rules of English.

English grammar includes a system of tense and aspect that indicates when actions take place and how they unfold over time. Tense refers to the time of the action, while aspect conveys how the action is related to the passage of time. Together, these elements are key to understanding the meaning of a sentence.

Tense: English has three primary tenses—past, present, and future.

Past: Describes actions that occurred in the past (e.g., "She walked").

Present: Describes actions that are happening currently or regularly (e.g., "She walks").

Future: Describes actions that will happen (e.g., "She will walk").

Aspect: English uses the perfect, progressive, and perfect progressive aspects to describe the state of an action in time.

Perfect: Describes actions that are completed relative to a point in time (e.g., "She has walked").

Progressive: Describes actions that are ongoing (e.g., "She is walking").

Perfect Progressive: Describes actions that have been ongoing up until a point in time (e.g., "She has been walking").

By combining different tenses and aspects, English speakers can convey detailed information about the timing and duration of actions, making communication more precise.

English grammar relies on agreement—the system in which elements in a sentence must match in certain features. One of the most important types of agreement is subject-verb agreement, which requires that the subject and the verb in a sentence agree in number (singular or plural). For example:

"She walks" (singular subject, singular verb)

"They walk" (plural subject, plural verb)

Another important type of agreement is noun-pronoun agreement. A pronoun must match the noun it replaces in number, gender, and person:

"John lost his keys." (The pronoun "his" agrees with the masculine noun "John.")

English grammar includes several sentence types, including declarative, interrogative, imperative, and exclamatory sentences, each serving a different communicative purpose.

Declarative sentences state facts or opinions (e.g., "I am going to the store").

Interrogative sentences ask questions (e.g., "Are you going to the store?").

Imperative sentences issue commands or requests (e.g., "Go to the store").

Exclamatory sentences express strong emotions (e.g., "What a beautiful store!").

In addition to sentence types, English allows for the use of various clauses (independent and dependent) to form more complex sentences. Independent clauses can stand alone as complete sentences, while dependent clauses need an independent clause to form a complete thought. For example:

Independent clause: "I went to the store."

Dependent clause: "Because I needed some groceries.

A. Word Order in English

Word order is another important aspect of English grammar. English typically follows a Subject-Verb-Object (SVO) word order in simple sentences. This means that the subject comes first, followed by the verb, and then the object. However, word order can vary depending on the type of sentence and the presence of other elements.

i. Questions

In English, questions often require an inversion of the subject and auxiliary verb (or modal verb) in order to form a correct structure. For example:

She is going to the store. (declarative sentence)

Is she going to the store? (interrogative sentence)

In the question, the auxiliary verb "is" comes before the subject "she." Similarly, modal verbs like "can," "should," and "would" are placed before the subject in questions:

Can you help me?

Should we leave now?

ii. Negative Sentences

To form negative sentences in English, the auxiliary verb (such as "do," "have," or "be") is used in conjunction with the word "not." In the case of a simple sentence, the negation is typically placed after the auxiliary or main verb:

She does not like coffee.

He is not coming to the party.

For questions, the auxiliary verb still comes before the subject, but "not" follows the auxiliary verb:

Do you not like coffee?

Is she not coming to the party?

iii. Imperative Sentences

Imperative sentences are used to give commands or make requests. The subject is typically implied rather than explicitly stated, with the verb appearing at the beginning of the sentence.

For example:

Close the door.

Please help me with this.

While the subject (you) is not mentioned, it is understood that the speaker is addressing the listener directly.

Other Structural Patterns

In addition to sentence structure and word order, several other structural patterns in English grammar help convey meaning effectively.

iv. Active and Passive Voice

In the active voice, the subject of the sentence performs the action, while in the passive voice, the subject receives the action. In English, sentences can be written in either voice, depending on the focus of the sentence.

Active voice:

The dog chased the cat.

Passive voice:

The cat was chased by the dog.

While the meaning of both sentences is similar, the focus shifts in the passive voice to the cat, the recipient of the action.

v. Direct and Indirect Objects

In English, a verb may take a direct object, which receives the action directly, and an indirect object, which indicates to whom or for whom the action is done. These objects typically follow the verb in a sentence.

For example:

She gave him (indirect object) a gift (direct object).

In this sentence, "a gift" is the direct object, while "him" is the indirect object, as it indicates who received the gift.

vi. Conditional Sentences

Conditional sentences express hypothetical situations and their possible outcomes. They typically follow a specific structure that includes an "if" clause (dependent clause) and a result clause (independent clause). There are different types of conditional sentences depending on the likelihood of the event occurring.

For example:

If it rains (if clause), we will stay indoors (result clause). (First conditional - real possibility)

If I had known (if clause), I would have helped (result clause). (Third conditional - hypothetical past event)

Conditional sentences reflect different degrees of certainty about an event's outcome.

Every language has a system or a structural pattern that is unique to its linguistic environment. It is true with all the living languages on the planet. By the word "living" what we mean are the languages that are still spoken and have an active user population and associated vocabulary. This might not include those that have gone extinct, like the Bo in the Andaman and Nicobar Islands. Of course, we can analyse a 'dead' language like Aramaic or even Latin to analyse its structure, but what would not be palpable is the language use at present and how it differs linguistically across cultures. For instance, English is a global lingua franca—it is a world language, but the varieties differ and sometimes the structural pattern. We Indians are often fond of using the present continuous tense, while Britons are not:---

Take two examples:

1.   Are you thinking that you might succeed? [Indian English]
2.   You think you might succeed? [British English]

Let us take into cognisance another variety of English, i.e., American English that is gaining ground and becoming popular. In American English, especially in the Afro-American variety, there is a pronounced tendency to use double negatives:

1.   I ain't got nothing man! [Afro-American Vernacular]
2.   I ain't done nothing to make a journey to Brooklyn. [-do-]

Notice the use of the double negatives "ain't" and "nothing"—structurally and syntactically, they would yield the impression that the speaker means something that is positive and affirmative, but that is not the case here. The use of double negatives here is to simply ensure that the effect is still negative, albeit in a more pronounced manner. Thus, the study of the structure of any language basically comes under the area of syntax or the arrangement of words in a language system that has both a syntagmatic function as well as a paradigmatic function. Combinations like the ones given below do not yield any meaning.

1. Got him and see
2. Hear did he and
3. Better be he aspire

The major problem with these sentence combinations is that they are unintelligible—one cannot make out what they mean simply because we are not attuned to using such patterns and syntactical arrangements. Simply speaking, the language system in English has a specific pattern, the basic being the S-P [Subject-Predicate] and the S-V-O [Subject-Verb-Object] pattern. Thus, the expression "Got him and see" does not mean anything simple because it does not cohere within any of these 2 patterns.

B. Surface structure and Deep structure approach

The celebrated American linguist and philosopher Avram Noam Chomsky (b. 1928) in his book *Syntactic Structures* (1957) postulated that any utterance within a language system has two levels: a surface as well as a deep structure. While the deep structure remains basically the same, the surface structure goes a kind of concatenation of sorts depending on the context and the needs and requirements of the situation. Consider the given sentence:

Ram woke.

It is a sentence of 2 words only, the proper name Ram and the verb in the simple past tense like woke. The sentence can get elongated as this,

- Ram woke and ate.
- Ram woke and ate a banana
- Ram woke, ate a banana, and went to the washroom
- Ram woke, ate a banana, went to the washroom, and came out [and so on...]

One noteworthy thing that can be observed here is that while the core sentence "Ram woke" remains the same, there is an immense possibility to add more units of information as seen in the examples above. This is, in simple terms, what Chomsky calls "surface" and "deep" structure—while the deep structure remains the same, the surface structure is capable of generating innumerable structures based on the requirements of the linguistic environment. Thus, while the surface structure remains the same, deep structures keep on changing and are capable of generating vast amounts of information and structural features.

C. **ICT or the Immediate Constituent Analysis Approach**

Another way of looking at the structure of a language system, particularly English is the ICT or Immediate Constituent Analysis. The approach was first used by the American structural linguist Leonard Bloomfield (1887-1949) and carried forward by Rulon Wells and had its full flowering in the early work of Noam Chomsky. This approach puts forward the basic idea that a sentence can be divided into a noun phrase (NP) and a Verb Phrase (VP) that is amenable to analysis of its constituent parts through a tree structure. As any kind of visual introspection would show, the sentence "This tree illustrates IC-analysis according to the constituency relation" has been broken down to first the NP and the VP and then, other parts of speech viz. an article, noun or determiner (shown by the letters D, A and N). The approach gained full momentum under Chomsky and is still in vogue today, although better 'models' that explain the language system have come up especially after the behaviorist and the cognitive revolution. George Lakoff (b. 1941) in his book *Metaphors We Live By* (1980) identifies key metaphorical patterns in our language use that we have now taken for granted but use them to explain our complex thought patterns on a day-to-day basis.

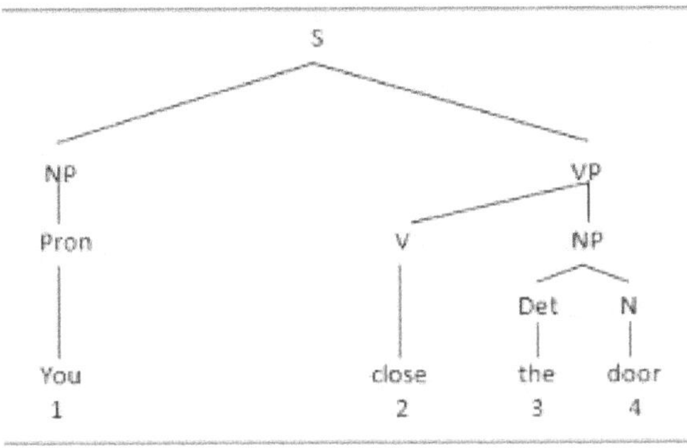

Courtesy: Deep Structure vs. Surface Structure | Awin Language

Self-Assessment Questions

1. The book *Metaphors We Live By* is authored by:

    i.   Avram Noam Chomsky
    ii. George Lakoff
    iii. Ferdinand de Saussure
    iv. Robin Lakoff

2. Avram Noam Chomsky's *Syntactic Structures* was published in the year:

    i.   1987
    ii. 1985
    iii. 1957
    iv. 1857

3. The IC Analysis was initially inaugurated by:

    i.   Zellig Harris
    ii. Leonard Bloomfield
    iii. Noam Chomsky
    iv. Marianne-Celce-Murcia

4. The expressions "surface structure" and "deep structure" were popularised by:

   i. Noam Chomsky
  ii. David Nunan
 iii. AS Hornby
 iv. None

5. The IC analysis of a sentence divides it into:

   i. A Noun Phrase and a Verb Phrase
  ii. A Noun Phrase and Adjective Phrase
 iii. An Adverb Phrase and a Verb Phrase
 iv. A Noun Clause and a Verb Clause

D. **Verbs**

It has been rightly pointed out that the verb is perhaps the most important and integral part of any sentence. It would not be an exaggeration to say that there cannot be a meaningful sentence without a verb. But then, how would the verb be defined?

In simple parlance, doing words are verbs. This means that any word or a phrase that denotes an action is done, is a verb. It comes from a Latin word "verbum" meaning a "word" — this is simply because it is considered the most vital word in a sentence. Consider the following sentences:

I love baseball.

I went to Chennai the other day. I hate you.

Get out of here!

In each of these sentences, the underlined words are verbs as they denote some action that is being carried out or accomplished. As per the Collins Dictionary, a verb is "a word such as ' sing', ' feel', or ' die' which is used with a subject to say what someone or something does or what happens to them, or to give information about them." Similarly, Wren and Martin in their High School English Grammar & Composition define verb as "a word that tells or asserts something about a person or thing. Verb comes from the Latin verbum, a word." Whatever the definition, it has been often seen that a verb occupies a medial position in a sentence:

He went for dinner I want ice cream

There is an alternative

If the verb were removed, the sentences would be rendered meaningless. Thus, the word "is" is a helping verb. A helping verb is a verb that helps the main verb to complete the sense in a sentence. For instance, in the sentence: "He is going to the market", the main verb is "going" while the helping verb is "is". If we remove the helping verb or auxiliary verb from the sentence, it would be ungrammatical and jarring to the ears.

i. Regular & Irregular Verbs:

Verbs and verb patterns may also be divided into two kinds: regular and irregular verbs. Let us see what this means. When we make a past tense of any verb, then it takes a different form and for the past participle, i.e., when the auxiliary has or have or had is used, it may or may not retain the form of the past:

REGULAR VERBS			IRREGULAR VERBS		
PRESENT	PAST	PART PARTICIPLE	PRESENT	PAST	PAST PARTICIPLE
beg	begged	Begged	be	Was were	Been
copy	copied	Copied	begin	began	Begun
dry	dried	Dried	break	broke	Broken
fit	fitted	Fitted	build	built	Built
hug	hugged	Hugged	choose	chose	Chosen
marry	married	Married	come	came	Come
plan	planned	Planned	Do	did	Done

Courtesy: Creative Commons

In these three instances, we can readily see that the simple past and the participle is formed by the mere addition of the "-ed" to the base form of the verb. However, this is not always the case, though in most cases, this is how we derive the simple past as well as the past participle forms. Regular verbs derive their past and past participle forms by the addition of the "-ed" to the base form. On the other hand, in case of the irregular verbs, the entire word changes and may also remain the same in all the three cases. Look at the following instances:

Here, as might be readily seen, the 2nd and the 3rd form of the verb changes in the last 3 examples and this is achieved not just by adding a mere "-ed" suffix to the base/root form, but by changing the entire word and its spelling. This is yet another form that irregular verbs might assume.

Let us use some of these verbs in sentences for a quick usage test:

- He became the captain of the team yesterday.
- He had become the captain of the team after the retirement-announcement of the previous captain.
- By the time he had finished his game, his mother arrived.
- I painted my door.
- I had painted my door a lot before it started raining.
- By the time I had painted my door, the tenant left.
- The ship sank in the Atlantic.
- The ship had already sunk in the Atlantic by the time the rescue arrived.

E. **Modals and Modal Auxiliaries:**

The word "auxiliary" means to help or assist—therefore, auxiliaries are basically helping verbs that help the main verb to complete its sense. As per Wren and Martin: "The verbs be (am, is, was, etc.), have and do, when used with the ordinary verbs to make tenses, passive forms, questions and negatives, are called auxiliary verbs or auxiliaries" (90). [1] Have a look at the sentence below:

- I am helping my brother carry on his responsibilities.

Here, the word "am" is the helping verb and the "helping" is the first primary verb and "carry" the secondary, though both are important to convey the sense to the reader. If the word" am" is removed from the sentence, it would convey little sense. Thus, this is an example of a helping verb or an auxiliary verb. They are also known as "modal auxiliaries". Thus, these verbs are known as modal auxiliaries:

can, could, may, might, will, would, might, will, would, shall, should, must and ought

These verbs are included in the group and in some grammars, as per Wren and Martin, they are also known as "modal auxiliaries". Let us look into some of the examples of the use of these helping verbs:

Be:

I am working in a bank.

Could:

Could I take a leave tomorrow?

Have:

I have to go to the market to buy some veggies.

Do:

He does not work here anymore.

Can:

He can do the work provided he has the time.

Could and Might:

He could have come to me to ask the same. He might have helped you.

Shall, Will:

Shall and Will are used interchangeably now—the fine distinction that 'shall' is used in the first person and will in all persons to express actions to be done in future is slowly being done away with.

I shall/will be going to meet the Dean of the College today.

I shall/will talk to the person concerned related to the admissions.

Should:

He should meet his teacher before it is too late.

Would:

'Would' is used in cases of a "polite case of want" (Wren and Martin 94): I would have helped her had she come to me.

The verb must agree with the subject in number and person, otherwise your sentences would be grammatically incorrect sentences.

Thus, Ram **sings**, but They **sing**.

Self-Assessment Questions

6. Will it be correct to say that a verb is the most important part of a sentence?

   i.   Yes
   ii. No
   iii. Cannot be determined
   iv. Partly yes and no

7. The past participle form of "cut" is:

   i.   Cut
   ii. Cutted
   iii. Cutting

iv.   None

8.   The past participle form of "rise" is:

   i.   Rise
   ii.   Rose
   iii.   Risen
   iv.   Rised

9.   The main difference between a regular and an irregular verb is:

   i.   There is a change in the spelling
   ii.   There is both a change in spelling as well as pronunciation
   iii.   There may not always be such changes
   iv.   All

10.   The past tense of "go" is:

   i.   Went
   ii.   Gone
   iii.   Going
   iv.   Goed

F. Voice

Along with verb and modal auxiliaries, the concept of voice is of cardinal importance for excelling in any communicative scenario, be it a corporate presentation or a simple talk with your employer regarding current issues. Voice may be defined as the manner or way a sentence gets told. Thus, when the form of the verb denotes that the subject is the active agent, we have instances of the active voice. Here, the subject is the active doer of any action. At the other end of the spectrum, when the verb denotes that the subject or the person or thing denoted by it is not the primary doer of action, we have instances of a passive voice.

Let us take two examples:

The man is building a boat.

The boat is being built by the man.

Notice that here, the subject becomes the object and vice versa. This is one way in which we can form passive voices from active voices. Another feature of the above-mentioned metamorphosis is that when one is supposed to report on any situation or incident, passive voice should be used. Look at the sentences below:

i. Active and Passive Voice

Active Voice Passive Voice

Obey your parents--- Let your parents be obeyed

The cat killed the mouse ---The mouse was killed by the cat

Ram loves Gita ---Gita is loved by Ram

I love my students ---My students are loved by me

Who opened the gate?--- By whom was the gate opened?

Why did he write such a letter? ---Why was such a letter written? by him?

In each of these instances, the active voice lays emphasis on the directness of the action being performed, while in case of passive, the indirectness of action is the point of emphasis.

There are some sentences that defy passive transformation. For example, "He went to the market", by the rules of transformation is expected to yield a sentence "Market is gone to by him" which makes no sense. Thus, not all active sentences can have a passive transformation.

You can see that passive voice is used in two cases, if the subject is known or unknown. In the first case, subject is known, so, the subject could be eliminated. In the second case, the doer of an action is not known, so, here also the subject could be eliminated.

For instance, Ravana was killed. Here, we all know who killed Ravana. So, we can omit Rama. The bill is passed by the parliament.

Here, the phrase 'by the parliament' does not add much meaning to the sentence.

Usually, bills are passed by the apex law making body, that is known to all. Hence, we can omit it.

We say -- the shopping mall is opened at 10 AM. Here, we do not know the person who unlocks the doors. So, we say, it is opened.

Self-Assessment Questions

11. "There are some sentences that defy a passive transformation." The remark is true as:

i. The transformed sentence often has no verb

ii. The transformed sentence often has no adjective

iii. The transformed sentence often has no determiner

iv. The transformed sentence often is ungrammatical and yields no sense.

12. The active voice of "Let your parents be obeyed" is:

i. Obey your parents.

ii. Your parents should be obeyed.

iii. Do not disobey your parents.

iv. None

13. "In a passive transformation, the subject becomes the object and vice versa." The remark is:

i. True

ii. False

iii. Cannot be determined

iv. Both true and false in some ways

14. The active-passive transformation for the sentence "The cat killed the mouse" is:

i. The mouse is killed by the cat

ii. The mouse has been killed by the cat

iii. The mouse was killed by the cat.

iv. None

15. "Along with verb and modal auxiliaries, the concept of voice is of cardinal importance for excelling in any communicative scenario."

i. True

ii. False

iii. Cannot be determined

iv. Both true as well as false

G. **Reporting on On-Going Tasks in the Corporate World**

Corporate and business environments call for a specialised kind of language use that is markedly different from the way we use language in day-to-day life. A conversation with our boss asking about the status of a project report or taking down instructions from a peer team regarding the suggestions advanced for the improvement of a product requires a specialised knowledge of technical terms and even jargon. Reporting is an activity that is of paramount importance as it takes into stock the latest information and what to do with that kind of data.

i. Reporting: Why, How and When?

As per Emily Heaslip in the blog *CO*, "an effective reporting structure also creates checks and balances to help ensure the business is compliant and staying on budget. [...] The purpose of an organisational structure is to define how your business is going to run—starting with three key elements: 1. Chain of command: how are tasks delegated, and how is work approved; 2. Span of Control: who manages which employees, and what tasks fall under that department's responsibilities? 3. Centralisation: Where are decisions made? Which people and departments have a say in each decision?" [2]

The key point here is the manner work is delegated and to what extent language and the proper grasp of the associated structures may help in the delegation of such works. This is of paramount importance and any miscommunication may hamper work delegation, failure to meet deadlines and the plummeting of output and hence, productivity.

The World Economic Forum in "It's the Future of Jobs Report 2020" lays special emphasis on the enhancing of human skills through education and the rightful use of meaningful work: "Developing and enhancing human skills and capabilities through education, learning and meaningful work are key drivers of economic success, of individual well-being and societal cohesion. The global shift to a future of work is defined by an ever-expanding cohort of new technologies, by new sectors and markets, by global economic systems that are more interconnected than in any other point in history, and by information that travels fast and spreads wide." [3]

A brief look at the above-mentioned statement makes it clear that the use of technology and the ever-expanding network of markets and economic systems is of paramount importance along with the mere use of the right structures of a language to report and delegate works in a business environment. Proper use of language has to be embedded within the conceptual grid of emergent technologies that will support and enhance productivity.

Grammarly has become a new tool for proof reading and millions are using this software to correct their language errors and thereby gain an upper hand when it comes to communicating in a professional environment. *Grammarly* uses AI or Artificial Intelligence to spot errors in spelling, punctuation and syntax and gives a percentage of fairness in writing. The software asks about the target audience and sets its own proof-reading mechanisms in tune with the same.

ii. Documentation in the Professional Scenario:

After having looked briefly into the ramifications of the use of technology vis-à-vis language use, we may take stock of the kinds of technical documents that are used in a business or a corporate setting. To report on 'on-going' tasks in such conditions, we often end up using the following:

i.   Memos
ii. Reports & Proposals
iii. Notices and Circulars
iv. Minutes of a Meeting

iii. Memos or Inter-Office-Memorandums

Memos or Inter-Office-Memorandums are used to transmit messages from one department or another in a particular organisation. For example, the Department of Quality Assurance of any company may transmit any message of importance to the Department of Sales and Promotion. Whatever the nature of the message and the subject matter, it should be short, to the point and eschew personal opinions. Many in-built formats are available online for ready use:

H. Reports and Proposals

Reports and proposals have basically the same internal structure with the exception that while reports deal with past incidents while proposals with what is being contemplated or proposed. Both are highly technical documents and need specialised knowledge and expertise to transmit the desired information to the readers. Both can run to hundreds of pages and are often published online on the websites of the organisations they are related to or may end in just a few pages. Longer reports and proposals are normally bound and are valuable sources of information. Many of them can be found in public as well as private libraries, the world over and numerous sites on the web may also yield useful sources. Reports like the one on the profits generated by say, *Coal India* from 2019-2021 are submitted to a higher authority for scrutiny and inputs. Any report basically has the following internal structure and is divided into annual reports, academic reports, sales/marketing reports, weekly reports and project reports:

A Cover Page
    Title Page
    Acknowledgements
    Certificate,
    Table of Contents,
    Summary or Executive Summary
Main Units
    Recommendations
    Conclusion
    Further Reading

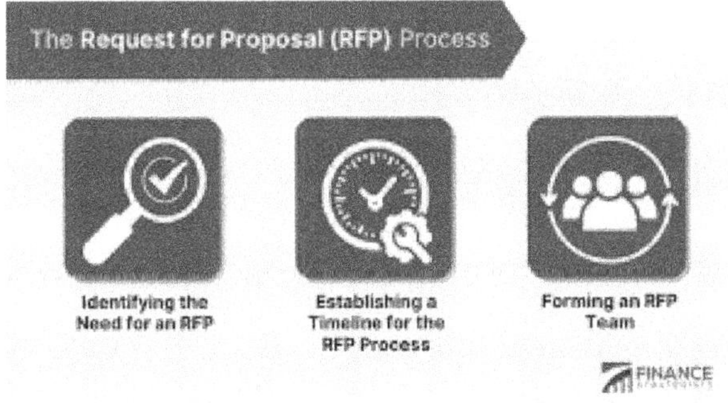

Courtesy: Creative Commons

I. **Notices and Circulars**

Notices and circulars are instances of short communication where the primary intention is to inform about an event. They are widely used in organisations throughout the world and can have a physical existence as well as a soft copy.

J. **Minutes of a Meeting**

Minutes of a meeting are again instances of information where the intention of the same is to record what is going on presently and can be best considered an example of a piece of information dealing with the ongoing tasks in a corporate or technical setting.

Self-Assessment Questions

16. As per Emily Heathslip, the levels of reporting on a structural level are:

    i.   1 in number
    ii. 2 in number
    iii. 3 in number
    iv. 4 in number

17. An Inter-Office Memorandum is meant for:

    i.   Internal circulation only
    ii. External circulation only.
    iii. Both internal as well as external circulation
    iv. None

18. Which of the following is not a part of a report?

    i.   Executive summary
    ii. Table of Contents
    iii. A letter to the editor of the report sent for review
    iv. Recommendations

19. Notices and Circulars are instances of:

    i.   Short communication
    ii. e-Communication
    iii. Long communication
    iv. None

20. Which of the following statements is not true about reports?

    i.   They are an instance of official communication

ii.   They basically have the same structure as that of a report
iii. They have exactly the same structure as that of a report
iv.   They need sufficient skill as well as expertise to be drafted.

Summary

Every language has a system of a structural pattern that is unique to its linguistic environment. It is true with all the living languages on the planet. Structural patterns include the internal structure o a language system: its syntax and the way different parts of speech cohere to form meaningful units of information.

A verb is perhaps the most important part o a sentence. They are classified into main verbs and auxiliary verbs, and into regular and irregular verbs. English has 23 pairs of auxiliary verbs, also called "modal auxiliaries".

Voice has to do with the mode of narration. It is of two kinds: active and passive voice. In the transformation from active to passive, the subject becomes the object and vice- versa.

Reporting about ongoing tasks in a corporate setting involves the use of written texts as documents. They need to be carefully written and executed as they follow a set structure and are a part o official documentation.

Some of such texts include memos, circulars, notices, agendas, reports and minutes of a meeting.

Reports and Proposals have basically the same structure with the major exception that the former report on past events and the latter on the future.

Minutes of a meeting, agendas and circulars are instances of short communications while reports and proposals are examples of longer corporate communications.

Terminal Questions

1. How would you define structural patterns in a language? Why do you think a working knowledge of structural pattern in English is of paramount importance along with one's ability to speak fluently?

2. "Understanding the kinds of texts and their function in day-to-day life is of cardinal importance". Do you agree with this view? Why or why not?

3. Why do you feel modals and auxiliaries are of paramount importance within the structural patterns of a language like English?

Activity

Activity type: Offline Duration: 40 Minutes
   Description:
Mr. Rajiv Verma works in a renowned manufacturing firm that assembles watches and wall clocks. He has been instructed by his boss to write a report on the dwindling sale of watches since 2019, coinciding with the onset of the COVID-19 pandemic. He has access to all the previous records of sales of watches starting right from 2010 in his company. His stable internet connection also allows him to access many other websites and databases that have to do with the sale of watches of every kind.

   Now answer the questions:

a. Why do you think Mr. Verma should consult external websites and databases to compile a report?

b. From this brief case study, do you think a report is an important official document and serves as a vital means of communication in a professional setting?

c. Design a mini report as per the specifications for Mr. Verma, highlighting the major sections and including relevant data. You could consider visiting https://visme.co/blog/ report-writing-format/ to generate ideas.

End Notes:

1. Emily Heaslip. "Buidling Your Team: How to Create an Effective Company Reporting Structure." *CO*. www.uschamber.com/co/run/human-resources/company

2. P.C. Wren & H. Martin (2007). *High School English Grammar & Composition.*
Rev. by N.D.V. Prasada Rao. New Delhi: Sultan Chand.

3. World Economic Forum. "The Future of Jobs Report 2020." P. 8. Retrieved from
https://www3.weforum.org/docs/WEF_Future_of_Jobs_2020.pdf.
Accessed 10 December 2024.

SHORT BIBLIOGRAPHY

External Resources

Martin, H. (2016). *Advanced English Grammar with Answers.* Cambridge University Press.

Raymond, M. (2013). *English Grammar in Use.* Cambridge University Press.

Kumar, S., & Pushpalata. (2015). *Communication Skills* (2nd ed). Oxford University Press.

Wren, P. C., & Martin, H. (2007). *High School English Grammar & Composition*. Rev. by N.D.V. Prasada Rao. S Chand.

Video links

Topic

Structural Patterns in English Grammar

https://www.youtube.com/watch?v=Y_ALOm0Ftbw

Verbs

https://www.youtube.com/watch?v=LciKb0uuFEc

Voice

https://www.youtube.com/watch?v=nRGLDD0BBdchttps://www.youtube.com/watch?v=nXNFyY7xe8I

Documentation in the Professional Scenario

https://www.youtube.com/watch?v=U_5xzub7z3khttps://www.youtube.com/watch?v=w-vvrcQdpZQhttps://www.youtube.com/watch?v=QjVPssAvyFMhttps://www.youtube.com/watch?v=EpRHZedSlz4

Keywords

Corporate communication

Modals and voice

Language system

Structural pattern

Immediate constituent analysis

CHAPTER FOUR

Investigating the Patterns

English grammar, as a structural system, reveals various qualitative patterns that help speakers convey meaning, organize ideas, and understand relationships between words and phrases. These patterns are not always rigid rules but rather recurring tendencies and conventions that shape the way language is used. From sentence construction to the subtle nuances of word choice, these qualitative patterns can be understood through an exploration of syntax, morphology, phonology, and semantics. Syntax refers to the arrangement of words in sentences, and one of the most noticeable qualitative patterns in English grammar is the Subject-Verb-Object (SVO) word order, which forms the foundation of declarative sentences in English. This basic syntactic structure enables speakers to convey clear, unambiguous ideas, where the subject performs the action indicated by the verb, and the object is the recipient of that action. For example, in the sentence "John (subject) kicked (verb) the ball (object)," the SVO pattern provides a clear meaning, establishing a relationship between the doer of the action, the action itself, and its outcome. In addition to basic word order, English also uses various syntactic structures to express different kinds of sentences, such as questions, negations, and commands. Questions, for example, often involve a subject-auxiliary inversion, where auxiliary verbs (like "do," "have," or "will") precede the subject, as in "Is John going to the store?" Negation typically involves the use of "not," often combined with auxiliary verbs, as in "John is not going to the store." Commands, on the other hand, tend to omit the subject entirely, focusing directly on the action, as in "Go to the store." These syntactic variations allow English speakers to adjust their communication style based on context and intention, with each type of sentence fulfilling a different role in discourse.

Morphological patterns in English grammar further enrich the language's qualitative dimensions. Morphology concerns the structure of words, particularly how smaller units of meaning, known as morphemes, combine to form words. English has both free morphemes, which can stand alone as words (e.g., "book," "dog," "run"), and bound morphemes, which must attach to a free morpheme to convey meaning (e.g., prefixes like "un-" in "undo," or suffixes like "-ing" in "running"). Through these combinations, English speakers can generate a wide array of word forms that communicate different aspects of meaning, such as tense, aspect, number, and possession. For example, the verb "to walk" can be modified morphologically to convey past tense ("walked"), ongoing action ("walking"), or future action ("will walk"). Similarly, English nouns can take plural forms by adding the bound morpheme "-s" (e.g., "cats"), or possessive forms by adding the suffix "'s" (e.g., "John's book"). These morphological patterns help organize grammatical relationships within sentences, enabling speakers to express various temporal, numerical, and possessive meanings. Phonology also plays a crucial role in the qualitative patterns of English grammar. Phonological patterns concern the sounds of language, and English features a range of sound patterns that influence how words are formed and pronounced. English phonology follows certain rules regarding stress patterns, intonation, and pronunciation that can impact the meaning of sentences. For instance, English uses stress to distinguish between nouns and verbs that are spelled the same but have different meanings. The noun "record" is stressed on the first syllable ("RE-cord"), while the verb "record" is stressed on the second syllable ("re-CORD"). Intonation, the rising and falling pitch of speech, also plays a key role in signaling different types of sentences or emotional tones. For example, rising intonation at the end of a sentence typically indicates a question, as in "Are you coming?"

In contrast, falling intonation often indicates a statement or command, as in "You're coming." These phonological patterns, while not part of the written grammar, are fundamental to how English speakers produce and interpret language in real-time communication. In addition to phonological and morphological patterns, qualitative patterns in English grammar can be found in its use of tenses, aspects, and moods. English has a relatively complex system of tenses, allowing speakers to convey different times of action (past, present, future) and nuances in the way actions unfold over time. The past simple tense, for example, indicates a completed action in the past ("She went to the store"), while the present continuous tense suggests an action that is happening right now ("She is going to the store"). The future tense, expressed with the auxiliary verb "will," indicates an action that will happen in the future ("She will go to the store"). Aspects such as the perfect aspect ("has gone") or progressive aspect ("is going") add further layers of meaning to the tense system, helping to clarify whether an action is ongoing, completed, or habitual. Moreover, English employs modal verbs like "can," "must," "should," and "may" to express various degrees of necessity, possibility, or permission, as in "She must go to the store" (necessity) or "She can go to the store" (possibility). These patterns in tense, aspect, and mood reflect how English grammar allows speakers to express subtle distinctions in time, modality, and intention. Semantics, the study of meaning, also reveals qualitative patterns within English grammar. English relies on a variety of strategies to express meaning, including word choice, collocations, idiomatic expressions, and metaphorical language. Word choice is central to these patterns, as speakers select words that carry specific meanings based on their context and purpose. For example, the choice between the verbs "say" and "tell" may seem subtle but carries different implications: "say" is often used when referring to something spoken, while "tell" generally implies giving information to someone directly. Additionally, English speakers often use collocations, or word combinations that are commonly found together, such as "make a decision" or "take a shower." These collocations follow qualitative patterns that are not arbitrary but reflect established conventions in the language. Idiomatic expressions, too, contribute to the richness of English grammar, as they use figurative meaning to express ideas in creative ways. Phrases like "kick the bucket" (meaning "to die") or "break the ice" (meaning "to start a conversation") add depth to language by playing on metaphorical meanings. These expressions follow patterns that native speakers recognize and understand, even though their meanings are not derived directly from the words themselves. The interplay of word choice, collocations, and idioms creates a complex web of qualitative patterns that shape how meaning is constructed and communicated. Finally, discourse-level patterns in English grammar are essential for understanding how language works in larger communicative contexts. At this level, grammar governs how speakers organize information in conversation or writing, guiding coherence, cohesion, and turn-taking. Discourse markers like "however," "therefore," "in addition," and "on the other hand" help signal shifts in thought and structure arguments logically. These markers follow predictable patterns that enable listeners or readers to follow the flow of ideas. Additionally, English discourse often follows a theme-comment structure, where the theme (the subject of the sentence) is introduced at the beginning and then commented on. For instance, in the sentence "The book (theme) was really interesting (comment)," the theme-comment structure allows the speaker to present new information clearly and effectively. Such patterns are integral to effective communication, whether in spoken or written language, and reflect the broader organizational rules that govern English grammar.

In conclusion, the qualitative patterns in English grammar are diverse and multifaceted, touching on every aspect of language, from the smallest phonetic units to the grander discourse structures. These patterns provide speakers with the tools to construct meaning, organize their thoughts, and express ideas in a coherent and contextually appropriate manner. Understanding these patterns is crucial for mastering English grammar and for appreciating the subtle ways in which language functions to reflect human thought and communication. Through syntax, morphology, phonology, and semantics, the language reveals a rich tapestry of structures that serve to organize and convey meaning, demonstrating the inherent complexity and beauty of English as a dynamic system of communication.

A. Qualitative Patterns and Structures

i. The adjective

What are qualitative patterns in a language system, especially in English? We all know what is quality — the epithet means that we attach a special significance to a thing or attribute that is considered useful, or we may just think about an undesirable quality as well. Thus, in everyday language use, we talk about such qualitative parameters. Examine the given sentences below:

Ram is an intelligent boy.

It's a sweet mango

The broad road leads to Chennai

A kind king forgave the offenders

In each of these sentences, we can readily see that the words "boy", "mango", "road" and "king" have been supplied with certain attributes. These are qualitative in nature—they talk about a quality that we hold dear, viz., kindness, sweetness and intelligence. However, we cannot measure them, they are not 'quantifiable' in any way. They are called adjectives that add to the description of a noun or a pronoun. And they are adjectives of quality or qualitative adjectives.

Again, examine the sentences:

He ate ten rotis

I have some sugar

The iron weighs ten kilograms.

He has ten sacks of wheat

In each of these sentences, we get a clear understanding about the quantity of the goods (here,

nouns) describes. They are quantifiable and hence are called adjectives of quantity. Thus, we have different kinds of adjectives, each describing a noun of a pronoun in a special way.

Adjectives, then are words that attribute a special status to either a noun or a pronoun. They are mainly of 4 kinds, with a 5th added and often classed as the same part of speech:

1. Adjectives of quality --- that describe an abstract quality, i.e., He was a kind king.
2. Adjectives of quantity --- that describe a quantifiable, i.e., I have some rice.
3. Adjectives of number --- that describe numbers, i.e., five fingers, two mangoes
4. Demonstrative adjectives --- that describe which person or thing is meant, i.e., This boy is weak.
5. Interrogative adjectives--- that ask a question specific to a person's attributes, i.e., Where is that lazy boy?

As you can see, adjectives are then qualifying words that either qualify a noun or a pronoun. We use a host of adjectives in our day-to-day lives and sentences will tend to have at least an adjective in one way or the other. There are also instances of adjectives clauses where a part of a sentence (a clause is a part of a full sentence with a subject and a predicate) shows some quality or attribute being recorded or an adjective phrase (a phrase is a part of a sentence that often does not make full sense and has neither a subject or a predicate). Since our discourse in daily lives incorporates these structural patterns, let us look at them in brief before moving into a more detailed discussion of the use of adjectives in business and allied settings: Ram woke.

ii. Adjective phrases:

The tax collector was a man **with a kindly nature.**

The chief lived in a **house made of mud.**

In each of the given sentences, the words in bold are just parts of a sentence that do not have either a subject or a predicate and qualify the tax collector and the chief, just as an adjective does. Thus, they are adjective phrases.

iii. Adjective clauses:

That man, **with a long stick,** is my brother.

The car, **with a broken windscreen,** belongs to Mr. Ravi.

In each of these two instances, the words in bold have a subject and a predicate of its own and do the work of an adjective. They are therefore adjective clauses.

iv. **The adjective: degrees of comparison**

After having looked at the definition of an adjective along with how to identify an adjective phrase and a clause, we may now turn over to the degrees of comparison. Simply speaking, you may say that "Ram is tall", but if Rahim comes and stands beside Ram who is shorter than Rahim, you say that "Rahim is taller than Ram." However, of Roshan comes, who is taller than both Ram and Rahim, you'd say that "Roshan is the tallest of all." This degree of comparison is a hallmark of adjectives and their use in day-to-day life.

Thus, the adjective "tall" belongs to category 1 or the positive degree, "taller" belongs to category 2 or comparative degree, and "tallest" to category 3 or the superlative degree.

Self-assessment question:

Consider this situation below:

Lucy has just joined a new organisation that specialises in marketing food products to Americans living outside the USA. After work, she has written an email to her pal Amanda about her experience, but has, out of sheer enthusiasm, committed visible mistakes in the degree of comparison of the adjectives. Correct them and you can also get connected with your friend online to indulge in possible pair work:

To: <u>amandarobins@outlook.in</u> From: <u>lucky0021@gmail.com</u>

Sub: Hi ! Let's chat.

Dear Amanda,

I just joined the **wonderfullest** organisation in USA when it comes to marketing, the FedMar Inc., Oklahoma. The colleagues there are **very better** than the last organisation where I worked. You have **extremely wonderful** flexible hours and by 4 PM, you're in your apartment. But Oklahoma is **hot** than New York City; it is also **cheapest** than either Florida or North Dakota. The task here is **lightest** than compared to my previous job and I get a free dessert as part of my 'bonus' every weekend from the office.

Like to hear from ya... Cheers!

Lucy.

B. **The Adverb**

Just as an adjective qualifies a noun or a pronoun, an adverb qualifies a verb, an adjective or

another adverb. Let us examine a few sentences below---

He walked quickly.

He is eating slowly.

You came again?

The grapes are very sweet.

In each of these examples, we can see that the words in the bold are modifying or affecting the meaning of a nearby word. In the first sentence, the word "quickly" tells how fast the person was walking. Similarly, in the third sentence, the word "again" gives an inkling of the fact that the person in question might have come before and is causing trouble to the speaker.

As you can readily see, the words in bold here are called adverbs. They are of many kinds and form an indispensible part of any conversational process:

I. **Adverbs of time**
II. **Adverbs of frequency**
III. **Adverbs of place**
IV. **Adverbs of manner**
V. **Adverbs of degree or quantity**
VI. **Adverbs of affirmation or negation**

VII. Adverbs of reason

i. Adverbs of time

As the name suggests, adverbs of time specify about a particular timeframe:

I think we met before in Shimla.

Rati fell from her bed yesterday.

History was formerly taught by Mr. Sharma.

ii. Adverbs of frequency

Adverbs of frequency tell us how frequently or in what succession does an event take place:

He committed the crime twice.

Your son often commits mistakes in Mathematics.

Once upon a time, there lived a king.

Thrice he was offered a crown, and thrice he refused.

iii. Adverbs of place

Adverbs of place indicate where did the action occur and with what consequences:

Sit here.

Is the Principal within?

The Dean is out of the building.

iv. Adverbs of manner

They show how the action has been accomplished, i.e., in what manner.

Ram runs fast.

Please speak slowly.

The man works hard.

v. Adverbs of degree or quantity

They give us an indication of to what extent or in what degree an action is perceived:

The grapes are almost ripe.

He is too carefree.

You're quite mistaken sir.

vi. **Adverbs of affirmation or negation**

They are words that emphasise either affirmation or negation.

Surely, you're lost.

We certainly met.

vii. **Adverbs of reason**

They are words that tend to explain a consequent action or comment additionally on such issues: The man is, hence, unable to report to duty today.

Therefore, we want you to leave.

Most of the adverbs end in "-ly". Thus, words like "slowly", "vastly", "easily" etc. are adverbs, though much depends on their position in a sentence.

Self-Assessment Questions

Fill in the blanks with an appropriate adverb.

1. She worked............................ and passed the examination.

   i.   Hard

  ii.   hardly

2. We............................ see a lion.

   i.   rarely

  ii.   scarcely

3. He narrated the incident in ....

   i.   detail

  ii.   details

4. He often comes............................... to school.

   i.   late

  ii.   lately

5. I really feel................................ about it.

   i. i. badly

ii. ii. bad

6. He is............................... rich.

i. very
ii. much

[Adapted from: *English Grammar.Org*]

C. **Time Expressions**

After you've looked into the kinds of adverbs that we use in daily parlance, we may now turn over to the concept of time expressions. Time expressions refer to the sentences and discourse that we use to reinforce the idea of a specific timeframe. This is evident as we humans perceive the world in terms of a viable timeframe. Works are executed and deadlines are set in terms of a time referent. However, a time referent is exactly not the same as a tense pattern as per The ESL Help! Desk. The source emphasises on the basic fact that humans are attuned to using a temporal time referent and this is how we view reality:

Time reference refers to when the action takes place, such as past, present, or future. This is a temporal concept in how human beings look at time and reality. Verb Tense refers to the particular grammatical form that the verb is in, such as simple past tense, future progressive tense, and past perfect tense. It is a grammatical construct. For example, in the sentence "My brother went out to play and didn't come back", the time reference is the past, and the verb tense is simple past tense. In other words, we are using simple past tense to express the past time reference.

So, what is a time referent? It is a more of an abstract concept, the myriad ways in which we tend to think about time and its nearing on day-to-day life of ours. We could have spent a holiday near a beach resort and numerous actions related to that two- or three-day stay may linger in our memory, but tense or "verb tense" is a more concrete grammatical form to realise that. Look at some of the examples below:

I went to the Cox Bazaar beach resort in 2019.

I remember walking on the sands then when I visited the resort.

I had a cup of green tea with a celebrity then.

I would have gone to the nearby beach had I not booked the tickets in advance.

If you have a look carefully at all the sentences, then it would be more than clear to you that all of them refer to an action that happened in the past, way back in 2019, but they use different verb-tense patterns of the past tense to realize the same. Thus, the time referent is past tense, but in order to clothe the same in grammatically correct forms, we are using different syntactic structures. Thus, we roughly have the same time referent, but the grammatical forms are different to express the fine slants in meaning.

Based on your understanding of time referents and the tense patterns in English from the earlier units, mark NTS for sentences that have different time referents and TS for sentences with more or less the same time referents. NTS= Not the Same; TS= The Same.

He used to go home at 5 PM. He went to home at 5 PM.

I went to Goa in 2015. I went to the Calangute Beach and has a fried salmon.

I was a topper in my HS exams. I had an A+ Grade then.

Mr. Rajesh will go to the US the next Fall. He will be going to the Louisiana State University.

D. Pronouns

Look at the given sentences:

I met Ravi. Ravi was out of station.

Shivaji was a great warrior. Shivaji defeated his enemies.

If you notice, you'll see that the first sentence has the proper noun "Ravi" twice that's jarring to the ears. This is also the case with the second sentence where the word "Shivaji" has been repeated again. We could rehash the sentence as follows:

I met Ravi who was out of station.

Shivaji was a great warrior who defeated his enemies.

The sentence sound much better now, don't they? Thus, a pronoun is a word that is used instead of a noun. Pronouns are of many kinds and it's worth noting some of them:

i. Personal Pronouns

They are the ones we use for addressing whether ourselves or a second person or third. Examples are:

I, you, we, they, it.

I like ice-cream

It is a nice puppy.

ii. **Reflexive and Emphatic Pronouns**

They are the ones used when the action done by the subject falls back on the subject itself: myself, yourself, ourselves.

He hurt himself.

If we quarrel, we divide ourselves.

iii. **Interrogative Pronouns**

They are the ones used to ask questions: who, whom, which.

Which is the house?

Who is there?

Whom do you want?

iv. **Indefinite Pronouns**

They are the ones used when we are not sure about the things we refer to in a general way:

one, none

One hardly knows what to say. None of the boys know this.

v. **Demonstrative Pronouns**

They are used to point out to a particular object or parameter referred to:

this, that, than

This bicycle has been imported from China. That is the Gateway of India. Indian lichis are sweeter than Chinese.

vi. **Distributive Pronouns**

They are used to refer to persons and things one at a moment.

each, either, neither

Each of you shall be awarded fifty thousand.

Neither of the charges are true.

vii. **Relative Pronouns**

They help in joining two statements and often do the job similar to that of a conjunction:

that, who

This is the car that I bought the last summer. He is Ravi who belongs to a rich family.

Self-Assessment Questions

Fill in the blanks with correct pronouns:

7. ------------ comes of a rich family.

   i. I

  ii. He

 iii. They

8. --------Ram--------- Shyam has any idea what to do.

   i. Neither, nor

  ii. Either, or

 iii. Both, together

9. house has a huge gate?

   i. That

  ii. Which

 iii. Whom

10. hardly knows this.

   i. One

  ii. None

 iii. No one

E. Conditionals

As the name suggests, conditionals refer to statements that are supposed to happen or will happen if a certain condition is fulfilled. They are one of the most widely use sentence structures used in any language, not to only mention English. Look at some of these sentences below:

If I had a lot of money, I'd travel round the globe.

If you add salt to water, it increases the boiling temperature.

You'll readily see, based on your understanding of a clause that the first part of the sentence is a conditional clause, as it contains a subject and a predicate. Thus, conditionals are usually clauses and form part of a sentence to drive home a condition based on which a subsequent action would be accomplished. As per Perfect English Grammar, conditionals are "if clauses" and they follow the given structure:

i. Zero Conditional

(if + present simple, ... present simple)
If you heat water to 100 degrees, it boils.

ii. The First Conditional

(if + present simple, ... will + infinitive)
If it rains tomorrow, we'll go to the cinema.

iii. The Second Conditional

(if + past simple, ... would + infinitive)
If I had a lot of money, I would travel around the world.

iv. The Third Conditional

(if + past perfect, ... would + have + past participle)
If I had gone to bed early, I would have caught the train.

Summary

Qualitative patterns include parts of speech like adjectives and adverbs that describe or provide us more information about the qualitative aspects of a statement. They help us determine to what extent the description of a situation or a state of affairs in a sentence is concerned about quality or a specific attribute.

Adjectives are qualifying words that either qualify a noun or a pronoun. We use a host of adjectives in our day-to-day lives and sentences will tend to have at least an adjective in one way or the other. Adjectives tend to have degrees, viz., the positive, the comparative and the superlative.

Adverbs qualify verbs, adjectives and other adverbs. They may even qualify an entire sentence. Adverbs are divided into adverbs of time, adverbs of frequency, adverbs of place, adverbs of manner, adverbs of degree or quantity, adverbs of affirmation or negation and adverbs of reason.

Pronouns take the place of nouns and are divided into kinds like reflexive pronouns, personal pronouns, emphatic pronouns and the like. They add ornament to a sentence when it comes to using them instead of proper nouns.

Time expressions refer to the action and the associated use of the tense structure. Time expressions are nuanced details of how our own perception is colored by the events and diurnal cycles.

Conditionals refer to sentences that rely on the fulfilment of any condition for the completion of the meaning. They are structured as zero, first, second and third conditionals respectively.

Terminal Questions

1. What are qualitative patterns in a language system? Explain their types.

2. "A skill to differentiate between the differences in the degrees of adjectives helps one gain more proficiency in a target language like English." Do you agree with this view? Why or why not?

3. What do you mean by conditionals? Do you feel they are important in the negotiation of meaning? Why?

Self-Assessment Questions

Activity

Activity type: Offline Duration: 40 Minutes
Description:
You are a company executive and have three employees, viz., Tom, Dick and Harry. Write a paragraph of around 500 words, describing their relative qualities, with respect to work, attitude and communication skills, with recourse to the degrees of comparison.

BIBLIOGRAPHY

External Resources

Helden, L. G. (1971). *BasicEnglishSentencePatterns*. Educators Publishing Service.

Hornby, A. S. (1997). *Guide to Patterns and U age in English*. 2nd ed. Oxford University Press.

Wren, P. C., & Martin, H. (2007). *High School English Grammar & Composition*.

Rev. by N.D.V. Prasada Rao. New Delhi: S. Chand.

Video Links

Topic

Qualitative Patterns

in English

https://www.youtube.com/watch?v=Wd5KRDi7Dzw

Adjectives

https://www.youtube.com/watch?v=laQUXyfVM9Y

Adverbs

https://www.youtube.com/watch?v=yFPS8yTS_Gw&t=36s

Conditionals

https://www.youtube.com/watch?v=bX7nTzbhOe4

Keywords

Language system

Adverbs and adjectives   Time expressions

Pronouns

Conditionals

CHAPTER FIVE

Navigating Workplace Communication

Workplace communication is a vital component of organizational success, facilitating the flow of information, enhancing collaboration, and fostering a positive work environment. Effective communication ensures that all members of a team, department, or organization understand goals, expectations, and roles, reducing the likelihood of misunderstandings and errors. It encompasses a wide range of communication methods, both verbal and non-verbal, as well as written and digital, and operates at multiple levels, from individual interactions to team discussions and organizational-wide messages. One of the most important aspects of workplace communication is clarity. Clear communication allows employees to know exactly what is expected of them and what they can expect from their colleagues. This is especially important in environments where tasks are interdependent and coordination is key.

Poor communication, on the other hand, can lead to confusion, inefficiencies, and frustration, potentially lowering morale and productivity. There are various forms of communication within a workplace, each with its advantages and drawbacks. For instance, face-to-face communication remains one of the most effective ways of conveying information as it allows for immediate feedback, the opportunity for clarification, and the use of non-verbal cues, such as body language and facial expressions, to enhance understanding. In contrast, email communication offers a written record and allows for messages to be thoughtfully composed and reviewed before sending. However, emails can lack the immediacy of face-to-face communication and may sometimes be misinterpreted due to the absence of tone and context. Meetings, too, are a common method of communication, but they can be time-consuming and inefficient if not properly structured. The balance between face-to-face, written, and digital communication requires careful consideration in order to maximize efficiency and ensure that the right medium is used for the right message.

Beyond the basic exchange of information, effective workplace communication also requires emotional intelligence. Being able to communicate with empathy, understanding, and respect fosters trust among team members and can lead to a more cohesive work environment. Conflict resolution is another critical area of workplace communication. In any organization, disagreements or misunderstandings are bound to arise, but how they are addressed can significantly affect team dynamics and morale. Open, honest, and respectful communication is crucial to resolving conflicts in a productive way. Additionally, feedback plays a central role in workplace communication, whether it's feedback from managers to employees, peer-to-peer feedback, or employee feedback to management.

Constructive feedback helps individuals and teams grow and improve while also promoting a culture of continuous improvement. Feedback, however, must be delivered thoughtfully and with consideration for the recipient's feelings and perspective to be most effective. Regular and clear communication from leadership is also essential to keeping employees aligned with the organization's mission, values, and goals. When leaders communicate transparently and frequently, they build trust and ensure that employees feel informed and engaged. Communication is equally important in remote or hybrid work environments, where teams may be geographically dispersed. In such settings, digital communication tools such as video conferencing, instant messaging, and project management platforms have become indispensable.

While these tools help bridge the physical gap, they can also introduce challenges, such as the potential for information overload, reduced personal connections, or difficulties in reading non-verbal cues. Therefore, remote workplace communication requires a balance of tools, thoughtful planning, and an emphasis on maintaining team cohesion and clarity. One aspect of workplace communication that is often overlooked is the role of organizational culture. The communication style and norms of an organization shape how information is shared and received. In hierarchical organizations, communication tends to flow in top-down channels, where decisions and instructions are often handed down from upper management to lower-level employees. In more collaborative or flat organizations, communication tends to be more open, with ideas and feedback flowing freely between individuals at various levels. The organizational culture also influences how employees communicate during informal interactions, such as during breaks or social events. These informal exchanges can provide opportunities for relationship-building and idea-sharing, which can contribute to a positive and productive workplace environment. Furthermore, communication in the workplace is not limited to internal exchanges. External communication, such as interactions with clients, customers, vendors, and other stakeholders, is equally important. Clear and professional communication with external parties reflects the organization's reputation and can impact its success. For instance, a company's customer service team must communicate effectively to resolve issues, address concerns, and provide timely updates to clients.

Similarly, clear communication with vendors is essential for ensuring the smooth procurement of goods and services. In these interactions, the ability to represent the organization's values, brand, and professionalism is key. Another important factor influencing workplace communication is technology. In today's digital age, technological advancements have revolutionized how communication takes place in the workplace. From emails and text messages to collaboration platforms and project management tools, technology allows for faster and more efficient exchanges of information. However, it also presents challenges, such as the potential for information overload or the risk of communication becoming too impersonal. Over-reliance on digital communication can sometimes hinder the development of personal relationships and a sense of connection between colleagues. Therefore, it's important for organizations to strike a balance between leveraging technology and fostering personal, face-to-face interactions.

In conclusion, workplace communication is a multifaceted and dynamic process that requires attention to clarity, empathy, feedback, and the appropriate use of different communication channels. Effective communication can enhance team collaboration, increase productivity, and improve organizational outcomes. Conversely, poor communication can lead to misunderstandings, decreased morale, and inefficiencies. Therefore, organizations must actively invest in developing communication skills at all levels and create an environment where open, respectful, and transparent communication is the norm. Ultimately, strong communication in the workplace is not just about exchanging information; it is about fostering relationships, building trust, and creating a culture of collaboration and shared purpose.

A. What are Formal Contexts?

We saw the myriad ways in which a working knowledge of grammar may help us communicate better in a professional context. Cognizance was also paid to the fact that this conception of having the rules of grammar up one's sleeves is open to debate as far as its applicability is concerned, but it must be accepted somewhere that grammar and its deft use in communicative events is needed for gaining proficiency in the target language, here English.

After the issue of grammar versus communicative competence, we may now turn our attention to the use of language and its associated dynamics in the professional sphere. You are, thus entering now into the realm of formal contexts. But, since it sounds big, it would be good to define this term "formal contexts."

Let's define by analyzing a set of situations first:

a. Mr. A is nervous. He is the chief sales marketing executive for Bosch and must deliver a presentation in front of a new clientele arriving from Kuala Lumpur.

b. Mr. S is going to a birthday party. He wears a pair of denim jeans and matching shirt and adds a generous quantity of the perfume "Lady Killer" as he has come to know that some of his female neighbors would be joining in as well.

c. Mr. F is a principal of a school, and he has to address the new batch of students who have joined his school along with their parents on the Republic Day.

Closely analyze the contexts or the 'backgrounds' of these three events. Which of these entails a much more attention to details and an adherence of the civic code? Do you think in all the three situations, the people mentioned can wear denims and wear flamboyant perfumes like "Lady Killer"? Why or why not?

As our little understanding of the matter tells us, there are situations where we need to be serious and adhere to some rules of the game. This does not mean that a funeral is a formal context. But while delivering a presentation, you can smile and even crack a joke to elicit audience attention. Thus, the line between formal and informal contexts looks to be a fine one. How do we know what makes a situation formal or informal?

You have to appreciate the fact that formal contexts are situations where you must adhere by certain norms specific to that context and the language to be used therein. This is called "register". A register is a specialized vocabulary used in a specific context. You might have seen court proceedings on the TV or even in real life when words like "objection", "My Lord" are used. However, you do not use such words in your home, but would only when they are to be used in a non-serious manner or for banter. Thus, formal contexts might be defined as communicative events that call for the employment of a vocabulary specific to the event. Thus, when you meet your friend, you do not use such formal terms but something else. Informal contexts are marked by the relative ease of language use and the slackening of power relations. This invariably means that formal contexts are highly structured units with a hierarchy. By "hierarchy", we mean the division of the workforce for better delegation of tasks. Look at the figure below that gives some idea about such a formalized structure and the hierarchy therein:

As per the site *peoplegoal*, "[f]ormal communication refers to the flow of official information through proper, predefined channels and routes. The flow of information is controlled and needs deliberate effort to be properly communicated. Formal communication follows a hierarchical structure and chain of command. The structure is typically top down, from leaders in various departments and senior staff in the organization, which funnel down to lower-level employees. Employees are bound to follow formal communication channels while performing their duties." [1]

Self-Assessment Questions

1. Formal contexts refer to:

   i. A tight hierarchy
   ii. An adherence to rules and regulations
   iii. Proper use of body language
   iv. All

2. As per the website *peoplegoal*, formal contexts have which of the given features?

   i. a top-down flow of communication
   ii. a bottom-up flow of communication
   iii. Both
   iv. None

3. "Formal contexts and informal contexts may sometimes coincide" --- the remark is:

   i. True
   ii. False
   iii. Partly true and false
   iv. Cannot be determined

4. What is a register in the communicative context?

   i. A specialized vocabulary used in a particular context.
   ii. A record of dry facts and figures
   iii. A ledger book used in a shop
   iv. None

5. You have to dress smartly to deliver a speech in a party thrown by your boss where many delegates would be coming for a get together before a training camp that will begin soon. The situation fits:

   i. A formal setting/context

ii.   An informal setting or context

iii.   Both partly

iv.   None

B. **What are Informal Contexts?**

i. **The Register**

We just saw that formal contexts operate within a particular hierarchy and setting. This means that formal contexts call for the employment of a particular discourse and register. You should know that a discourse is any use of language, written or spoken, within a setup or a context. This means that a discourse is language and setting specific. We just saw that formal contexts are "You have to appreciate the fact that formal contexts are situations where you must adhere by certain norms specific to that context and the language to be used therein." This means that informal contexts are supposed to be very different and are deemed opposite of the formal situations. Thus, informal contexts can be deemed less serious and demanding. Let us see how:

A.   Consider a situation where you have called your Boss to dinner. In this context, you can also read a much-anthologized story by Bhisma Sahni called "The Boss Came to Dinner." This will be a peculiar situation where you'll encounter a mixture of both formal as well as informal contexts. This is true as your boss will not be in a much demanding mood as he is supposed to be in his office. He'll be visiting your home along with his wife, as it happens in the story mentioned just now. Again, you need to be careful that none of your eccentricities should irk him, as he is a guest of the highest order. Any mistakes here can be suicidal for your career.

B.   What do you see here? Let's analyze a bit of the tale by Sahni. In the story, the Boss is an American who is invited by an employee Mr. Samnath for dinner, presumably for promotion. Though he and his wife do eat non-veg, his old mother is a pious country woman whom Mr. Samnath wants to hide to avoid any shame. He tells his mother to be inside a room and urges her rather unkindly not to come out till the Boss is gone. To add to the flavor of the party, a mini-bar is also improvised within the drawing room. But as ill-fate (if that be the word to describe this) would have it, the Boss meets the old mother, and is amused by her country ways. She evens sings and gifts a piece of village embroidery, called "phulkari" in the narrative. This adds spice to the evening which would, after all, have gone bland and flavorless.

C. **The context**

As per the site *One Team,* "Formal communication refers to the exchange of information or messages following official rules, policies, and hierarchical structure within an organization. It is characterized by the use of formal language, predefined communication channels, adherence to specific formats, and an overall formal tone." [2]. Thus, the definition brings home to us the following points about formal communication:

A. Official rules, policies

B. Hierarchical structure

C. Formal language

D. Predefined communication channels

At the other part of the spectrum, informal communication, as defined by *PeopleGoal*:

"is a type of casual and not formal communication that can take place between two or a group of individuals in the workplace or outside the workplace. The exchange of information is typically unplanned and impromptu. These types of conversations or discussions are not aligned to the official rules of communications of an organization. Anyone can be part of an informal communication and often enough it's difficult to define the start and end of the conversation." [3].

What do we see here? Communication is diverse and multi-faceted in nature and one cannot dissect all its trends. This means that we need to pay a close look at the context or the surrounding that envelops any kind of a communicative event. For example, had the Boss been equally stern at Mr. Samnath's house as he is in the office, things would have looked out of the way and even rude. Moreover, he was accompanied by his wife who would be eager to have a more relaxed and a lighthearted conversation. Again, Mr. Samnath cannot be too carefree with his Boss who would be inwardly eager to inspect him out of a formal context as well. Thus, the scenario gives us a feel of both a formal as well as an informal setting. This means that real world situations are a blend of such situations.

While there is a propensity to stress more on formal communication systems, informal communication is an area that often is relegated to the rear. We often feel that formal communication is more needed for professional growth, but this can be a myth that needs to be busted. As per an insightful article by Dr. Radhika Kapur entitled "Informal Communication Systems", informal communication is also very vital as it gives us a sense of professional excellence and job satisfaction. This means that informal communication is as vital as formal communication:

Within educational institutions as well as various types of organizations, it is necessary for the members to form amiable terms and relationships with each other. They need to be friendly in nature and promote mutual understanding. The reason being, they need to work in co-operation and integration with each other. In order to achieve professional goals, and incur the feeling of job satisfaction, it is necessary for the members of the organizations to get engaged in informal communication. In the implementation of informal communication, they do not follow any specific rules and procedures. Furthermore, the individuals communicate with each other in terms of various other topics as well, which are not work related.

Yet, as the researcher makes it clear, it is also very vital to maintain ethical standards vis-à-vis morality and communicative ethics. This is understandable as communication might involve inter-gender and inter-cultural communication that necessitates taking into account the inescapable fact that we need to be very careful as regards the expectations of the people on the other side. Usually, as common sense stipulates, we should be wary to ask (and disclose) the following points even if we are close to people in a professional setup:

1. Salary
2. Age (in case of opposite gender)
3. Caste or community

The list is just indicative and there can be other such parameters. Informal communication indeed gives a feeling of job satisfaction in the workplace, but it has to be a just blend of both the models of communication.

Formal Communication

Purpose

Conveys official information such as policies, procedures, regulations, etc.

Mainly used for social interactions like sharing personal experiences.

Structure

Follows a pre-established design

Free-flowing and unstructured

Tone

Professional

Casual

Channel

Uses official channels like memos, reports, etc.

Uses channels like face-to-face conversations, social media, etc.

Audience

Directed towards all employees or a particular department

Directed towards different audience groups comprising specific individuals or groups

Documentation

Needs to be documented as meeting minutes or email archives

Can be done without documentation for future reference

Authority

Often received from an authoritative position like a manager or an executive

Among peers

Consequences

Results in serious consequences like disciplinary actions or legal liability if not strictly followed

Does not have such serious consequences but may disrupt workplace relationships

Use of Language

Uses jargon or technical terms in abundance

Mostly uses slang specific to the workplace.

Some quotations:

"Communication is a skill that you can learn. It's like riding a bicycle or typing. If you're willing to work at it, you can rapidly improve the quality of every part of your life." — Brian Tracy

"To effectively communicate, we must realize that we are all different in the way we perceive the world and use this understanding as a guide to our communication with others." — Anthony Robbins

"Speech is our primary means of communication. If it's important, we tell people about it." — Brian Knapp

Self-Assessment Questions

6. The full form of a PA is:

    i.   Private assistant
    ii. Primitive assistant
    iii. Picnic assistant
    iv. None

7. What did Harry Houdini say about his personal assistants?

    i.   That they were a nuisance
    ii. That they were also responsible for his success
    iii. That they were responsible for his failure
    iv. None

8. What is yet another term loosely used for a PA?

    i.   An HR
    ii. An Office boy
    iii. The Dean
    iv. None

9. Which of the following is not a problem faced by the HRs worldwide?

    i.   Sexual harassment
    ii. Burn out
    iii. Good salary and perks
    iv. None

10. Which of the following is one of the jobs of a PA?

    i.   Maintaining inter and intra office communication

ii.   Keeping files and associated stuff in order
iii. Fixing appointments
iv.   All

D. Telephonic Conversation: Issues

i. The phone as an instrument

Over the years, the telephone, especially the cell phone has emerged as a powerful means of communication in formal settings. Though considered an outdated method of communication by mainstream critics of communication, the phone can become a powerful means of communication in a workplace. However, since the advent of social messaging services like *WhatsApp* that provides a host of services like instant messaging, telephone and mobile sets have been relegated to the rear. If the phone is used effectively, it can emerge as a powerful instrument of effecting change and positive vibes in a professional setting. Phone interviews are conducted by major companies nowadays to quickly interview people and select them. Taking orders over the phone is basically about communicating well and transacting the business successfully using good negotiation skills within the formal context using proper etiquette. But then, what are those "etiquettes"?

ii. Phone etiquettes

Though the phone can be used to its maximum possible extent in any communicative event, there have been instances where the misuse of the same can lead to hindrances in the workplace. One of the common ways of understanding this situation is to visualize a situation where a unit of an organization constantly keeps on calling another unit instead of using less 'disruptive' means like emailing or even Whatsapping them.

As per Readygrad, no matter whom we do call, it is important to learn proper phone etiquettes so that we may be able to give a good impression of the organization that we represent. Even though you are not visible over the phone, it is good to smile as the same would be reflected in your words. Many organizations have online resources to help you learn phone etiquettes within the larger discourse of corporate or professional communication.

iii. The Dos and Don'ts of telephonic conversation

Like any software package or a hardware component, the telephone or cell phone can either aid you in your professional setup or damage the cohesive working culture. This brings us to the Do's and Don'ts of telephonic conversation. No matter whom we call, either our friend or the boss, it is important to keep in mind the context. If it is formal, like in the latter, you need to choose words carefully. This is not to say that you would be too queasy while talking in a formal context and that too over the telephone that may give one an inkling of your confidence levels, if not your facial expressions. The Common Do's of a telephonic conversation in a formal setting are, if not limited to:

    i. Greet the person. If it is a woman, use "madam", if a man "sir." More informal greetings are allowed later, depending on context.

    ii. If you are a PA, and the person calling wants somebody, politely say "S/he is not here at the moment...may I take a message?"

    iii. If you are calling on behalf of a company, introduce the same in not more than 15 seconds and come to the point.

    iv. Do tell the person who has called you for a clarification that s/he would be contacted within 2 working days at most.

    v. If you are conducting a phone interview, listen to the other side and then proceed. The similar action is expected from the other end as well.

    vi. Speak clearly and avoid fumbling. If you are nervous, better postpone the call and try again later.

The common Don'ts are:

i. In a formal context, do not start your conversation with a "hey" or "hi". Better use such expressions at your own risk.

ii. Do not hang the phone for a long time. If you're using intercom, be sure that the other person should be available to answer back. Do not keep a prospective client waiting.

iii. Do not be unclear and fumble over the phone.

iv. Pick up the call within 4 rings and if needed, be apologetic that you could not pick up due to unforeseen situations and things beyond your conscious control.

v. Do not shout or whisper. Some people have the vague idea that whispering shows that you're humble, and shouting means you're confident. Nothing could be more far from the truth

Self-Assessment Questions

11. What are you not expected to do while talking over phone in a formal situation?

   i. Shout
   ii. Whisper
   iii. Both
   iv. None

12. When did Antonio Meucci file a patent in US Patent Office?

   i. 1874
   ii. 1875
   iii. 1871
   iv. 1885

13. Taking orders over the phone is all about:

   i. Right attitude
   ii. Correct phone etiquette
   iii. Both
   iv. None

14. You should hang the phone when someone calls you. The remark is:

   i.   True
   ii. False
   iii. Depends on the situation
   iv. None

15. "Phones calls are frequently used in interviews" --- the remark is:

   i.   True
   ii. False
   iii. Partly true partly false
   iv. The question needs a review.

E. Describing Changes in the Business Context

i. What is change?

Change is the only constant. There is no denying the fact that changes are desirable in a globalized as well as a glocalized world of today. This means that the business ecosystem can see these changes at any point of time, keeping in mind the various levels within an organization or a business situation. This has to be borne in mind that mergers are very common in today's business world where companies merge to get the best of each other. This has also become very common in the banking sector where banks often get merged, so do employees, funds in stock and expectations. One very common example is the recent merging of two banks in India—the United Bank of India and Punjab National Bank. With changes like these come changes in language patterns, vocabulary and even customer expectations. One very common example as regards the banking sector merger is the discourse employed by both the banks—while United Bank of India calls one's savings account as "Savings A/C", PNB is more attuned to call it "Savings Fund." This might create some confusion in the minds of the users and customers.

ii. Is Change needed?

As per *Haiilo*, people and even organizations are resistant to change. As per a research, a mere 38% people like to leave their comfort zone. But changes are needed in an organization for three primary reasons:

a. To implement new policies
b. To maximize resources
c. To reformulate existing core policies and values.

iii. Change vis-à-vis language use

As we saw in the previous sub-unit, changes are needed. This is necessitated by the changing business scenarios, global cash flows and economy as well as the flux that calls for a reorganization of the entire vision or mission of an organization. This also means that companies and organizations go for a merger when there are pressing needs to reorient; this could be with recourse to cash flows, sick units that are often 'taken over' by more financially sound organizations and other parameters.

Let us now have a look at the sample text from two organizations and their language use. This is evident from real-world experience that organizations that take over another organizations will use a language that it deems fit and 'proper' in a business context.

Company A

"This is for the information of all concerned that a café cum restaurant has been opened in the premises of our company. It has been observed since a long time that our valued employees have to depend on outside food that often was not hygienic. Moreover, going outside wasted man hours that could be out to good use for their personal growth and development. Thus, this café cum restaurant is sure to prove a boon for all of us."

Company B

"This is to inform all that employees cannot go out to have lunch every now and then. We have been suffering as regards man hours and efficiency. This has come to the notice of the top management that is taking the matter seriously. Please have food in the newly opened restaurant cum café. This is for strict compliance."

Ask yourself these questions:

i. Which company fares better when using appropriate language? Why?

    ii. Which company, it looks to you, is more attuned to accept change? Why?

    iii. Which company is clearer in formulating new policies and gathering support? A or B?

Self-Assessment Questions

16. As per an estimate, what percentage of people are likely to leave their comfort zones?

    i. 90%
    ii. 20%
    iii. 38%
    iv. 5%

17. "Change is inevitable and bound to happen across organizations" --- the remark is:

    i. True
    ii. False
    iii. Cannot be determined
    iv. Partly true and false

18. Which one of the following is a valid reason for changes to take place within a professional setup?

    i. To implement new policies
    ii. To reformulate new ones
    iii. To maximize resources
    iv. All

19. "Proper language use is a must when a change happens" --- the remark is:

    i. True
    ii. False
    iii. Cannot be determined
    iv. Partly true and false

20. The largest merger of two companies in history was in the year ---

    i. 2011
   ii. 2020
  iii. 2000
  iv. 2022

Summary

Formal contexts refer to the situations where one must adhere by certain norms specific to that context and the language to be used therein. This is called "register". A register is a specialized vocabulary used in a specific context.

A PA is a person who is entrusted with the task of delegating works related to office work in a particular organization. PAs are often tied to their bosses—high-flown executives who need someone to delegate jobs and make things easier.

Over the years, the telephone, especially the cell phone has emerged as a powerful means of communication in formal settings. Though considered an outdated method of communication by mainstream critics of communication, the phone can become a powerful means of communication in a workplace.

Changes are bound to happen across organizations for three primary reasons

1. To implement new policies
2. To reformulate new ones
3. To maximize resources

Terminal Questions

1. What are formal contexts? How are they different from informal ones? Provide examples.

2. What are the responsibilities of a PA? To what extent has s/he to be careful about language use?

3. Why are changes needed across organizations and how language use here plays a role? Discuss.

Activity
Activity type: Offline Duration: 40 Minutes
Description:
Suppose you are the chief marketing officer of a company that manufactures watches. You have to give a presentation before the board of directors regarding the low sale of watches during the COVID-19 pandemic and suggest solutions.

Make a list of things that you need for this formal occasion. This could include anything from your dress to tools for presentation. You can search the internet to get an idea. For example, one has been done for you. You could go for a discussion with a co-learner as well. Compare the points you both list and note the differences, if any.

a. A coat and pant with a matching tie as it is winter

b. A collar mike

End Notes:
1. *Peoplegoal.* "What is formal and informal communication?" https://www.peoplegoal.com/blog/what-is-formal-and-informal-communication. Accessed 10 May 2024.

2. *One Team.* "Formal Communication: Definition and Tips to Improve." https//:www.oneteam.io/en/blog/what-is-formal-communication. Accessed 15 September 2024.

3. *Peoplegoal.*

BIBLIOGRAPHY

External Resources

Cappelen, H., & Dever, J. (2016). *Context and Communication.* Oxford University Press.

Helden, L. G. (1971). *Basic English Sentence Patterns.* Educators Publishing Service.

Wrench, J. S. (2013). *Workplace Communication for the 21st Century.* Praeger.

Video links

Topic

Formal contexts

https://www.youtube.com/watch?v=egtyq2ccCIA

https://www.youtube.com/watch?v=knUEdy-kOIQ

A PA Within a Formal Context

https://www.youtube.com/watch?v=TgLh9lSWX_4

https://www.youtube.com/watch?v=sowvos090ew

Telephonic conversation

https://www.youtube.com/watch?v=x5KFZAB74_w

Changes in a Company and Language Use

https://www.youtube.com/watch?v=e4kYvMEQU3w

Keywords

Formal communication

Communicative competence

Language dynamics

Flow of information

Communication skills

CHAPTER SIX

The Essential Writing Kit You Need

A. Why a "tool kit"? Don't We Have Enough?

You must have heard of tool kits belonging to people like basic sciences, archaeology and other allied fields. In such cases, what does a tool kit do—it consists of some basic implements that help with the task. Like, in case of archaeology, you have small chisels, brushes and hammers that help with digging and pruning. Similarly, in case of writing and editing help, as well as with everything related to communicative competence, you need the following verticals to succeed:

- Essential vocabulary
- Idea of basic grammar
- Set words and phrases for official communication and documentation
- Sound idea about body language and workplace etiquette

B. Brushing Functional Grammar

Functional grammar, a branch of linguistics, focuses on how language is used to achieve specific purposes. It emphasizes the relationship between language form and its function, making it a powerful tool for understanding and improving communication.

One of the key advantages of functional grammar is its ability to explain how language is used in different contexts. By analyzing the choices people make in language, functional grammar reveals how language is shaped by social, cultural, and situational factors. This understanding is crucial for effective communication, as it allows individuals to adapt their language use to different audiences and purposes.

Furthermore, functional grammar provides a systematic approach to language analysis. It offers a framework for examining how different linguistic elements work together to create meaning. This framework can be applied to a wide range of texts, from simple conversations to complex academic writing. By understanding the underlying structure of language, individuals can become more skilled at producing clear, concise, and persuasive communication.

In addition to its practical applications, functional grammar also has theoretical significance. It challenges traditional views of grammar as a set of fixed rules and instead emphasizes the dynamic and flexible nature of language. By focusing on how language is used to create meaning, functional grammar offers a more nuanced and comprehensive understanding of the human language system.

Functional grammar, a linguistic framework, delves into the intricate relationship between language form and its communicative function. It offers a comprehensive analysis of how language is employed to construct meaning in diverse contexts. Central to this framework are several key parameters that shape our understanding of language use.

One fundamental parameter is the distinction between field, tenor, and mode. Field refers to the subject matter or topic of discourse, influencing the choice of vocabulary and technical language. Tenor, on the other hand, pertains to the social relationships between participants, impacting the level of formality and politeness. Mode, the third parameter, encompasses the channel of communication, whether spoken or written, and the medium used, such as face-to-face interaction or digital text. These three parameters interact to determine the overall register of language, guiding the selection of linguistic resources to achieve specific communicative goals.

Within the realm of functional grammar, the concept of clause as exchange is pivotal. A clause is viewed as a communicative event involving participants who exchange information. This perspective highlights the interactive nature of language, where speakers and writers construct meaning through the interplay of linguistic choices. The clause is analyzed in terms of its mood and residue. Mood refers to the grammatical structure that signals the speaker's intention, such as declarative, interrogative, or imperative.[10] The residue, on the other hand, comprises the remaining elements of the clause that convey the propositional content.

Furthermore, functional grammar emphasizes the importance of transitivity. This parameter explores how language is used to represent processes and participants involved in those processes. Transitivity involves the analysis of the verb and its associated participants, such as the Actor, Goal, and Beneficiary. By examining the different types of processes, such as material, mental, and relational, functional grammar sheds light on how language constructs our understanding of the world.

In conclusion, functional grammar offers a rich and nuanced framework for understanding language use. By considering parameters such as field, tenor, mode, clause as exchange, and transitivity, we can gain insights into the complex ways in which language shapes our thoughts, feelings, and interactions with others. This knowledge empowers us to become more effective communicators, capable of adapting our language use to diverse contexts and achieving our communicative goals with precision. Functional grammar is a valuable tool for understanding and improving communication. It helps us understand how language is used in different contexts, provides a systematic approach to language analysis, and offers a more nuanced understanding of the human language system. By embracing functional grammar, individuals can become more effective communicators and critical thinkers.

Please refer to the initial chapter on introductory grammar for more details on the tool kit.

C. **The ambience in writing**

There is no denying the fact that writing, especially effective writing creates its own ambience. By 'ambience', what we mean is the deft arrangement of sentences, the use of proper discourse features, idea of the register to be used as well as the use of right vocabulary. Though there is no right or wrong vocabulary, what we mean here is the use of a language that highlights non-archaic language, free from gender bias and using the vocabulary that one can associate with the new and current lexicon in a language system during a particular point of time. Though there are no accepted rules for this, good ambience in writing boils down to a few principles:

> i. Use of language that is free from common mistakes that are normally discernible.
> ii. Keeping words in their best use
> iii. Using non-sexist language

> iv. Using language that is free from ethnic slur
> v. Perceptible avoidance of jargon

As already pointed out, ambience is something that cannot be easily defined, but we can certainly mark a few features that count as 'effective writing'. But certain habits do indeed help us.

Ambience, the intangible atmosphere that surrounds a piece of writing, is a potent tool that can elevate a story from ordinary to extraordinary. It's the emotional undercurrent that flows beneath the surface, subtly influencing the reader's experience. By carefully crafting the ambience, writers can evoke a wide range of emotions, from tranquillity to terror, joy to sorrow.

One of the primary ways to establish ambience is through the use of vivid descriptions. By painting a picture with words, writers can transport readers to different worlds, immersing them in sights, sounds, and smells. For instance, a dimly lit room with a flickering candle can create a sense of mystery and foreboding, while a sun-drenched meadow can evoke feelings of peace and contentment.

The choice of language also plays a crucial role in shaping ambience.[3] The use of evocative words and figurative language can enhance the emotional impact of a scene.[4] For example, instead of simply stating "it was dark," a writer might describe the darkness as "a thick, inky blanket that smothered the land." This heightened language creates a more immersive and evocative experience for the reader.

Furthermore, the pacing and rhythm of the writing can significantly impact the ambience. A slow, deliberate pace can create a sense of suspense and anticipation, while a rapid pace can generate excitement and urgency. By varying the sentence structure and paragraph length, writers can control the ebb and flow of the narrative, manipulating the reader's emotions.

Ambience is an essential element of effective writing. By carefully crafting the atmosphere, writers can create a more engaging and memorable reading experience.[8] Whether it's a serene pastoral scene or a chaotic urban landscape, the power of ambience lies in its ability to evoke emotions and transport readers to other worlds.

By "ambience", we mean is the flow of words and language that is being written. This means that just as a room or setting generates its own ambience, so does a text. But how?

Texts generate their own ambience through the employment of apt vocabulary, current usage, use of jargon-less expressions and correct grammatical rules. This is a difficult task as English as a language, like any language is ever evolving with new lexicon. We also need to keep in mind the basic fact that no writing is complete in itself and that that are all amenable to editing. However, some steps can be naturally followed:

a.Use a consistent tense throughout: This means that we should preferably (though not always) stick to just one tense. Imagine using a medley of present, past and future tenses in a single paragraph! This would create a messy outlook and mar with meaning:

"I am right now studying the fact that Neanderthals are not so stupid as we thought about them. They were, actually, very smart and have been practicing elaborate burial customs. I read about them in a book published by the Nat Geo, that has told us that they will be seen as an intelligent species later on......."

As you can see here, meaning is interrupted by the description of these hominids who are a past, but the impression gathered by a reader is that they might still be living round the corner. Here, we see a curious medley of the mixture of all the three tenses. Though it does not destroy the meaning intended by the writer, it definitely is jarring to the senses.

b. Use simple and lucid language: Use of language that is understood by even a lay reader increases the readability of the passage. Any word that is confusing and engages in double speak should be avoided.

c. Avoid using a language that is sexist and ethnic: We should pay special attention to the fact that language has be to free from gender-bias and also without any ethnic slur. This means that phrases and words that smack of any of these should be done away with. Using a gender-neutral language is always welcome and enhances the readability of the article.

D. The "jerks"—Jargon, Johnsonese and Journalese

We all know what a jerk is. Jerk means any kind of disturbance. Or it may also imply some kind of an annoying or disturbing element that could be present in a language system. We have speed breakers on the road that act like jerks. Jerks can also be had if we do find potholes on a road. Similarly, there can be 'potholes' in writing. This means that there can be some elements in the passage or text that might be jarring to the ears. Thus, the language is robbed of its lucidity and flow, which means that it can be quite unwelcome to a discerning reader. Let us see what are those elements that can rob a language system of its spontaneity:

i. **Jargon:**

A jargon is an expression that refers to a technical term or likewise that might not be understood by the general population that one intends it for. This might refer to casual statements, short and set phrases and scientific terms. Though quite a welcome part of common conversation, jargons are often seen to be intrusive and annoying. Just have a look at the following sentence:

"Lol, pfa FYI the result of the boy! Tc."

This sentence contains many issues as regards comprehension. For example, how many of us are aware of the epithets "Lol" (laughing out loud), "FYI" (for your information), and "Tc" (take care)?

We may hope not many know. This is one example of how jargons can spoil the beauty of a sentence and the mechanics of comprehension.

ii. **Johnsonese:** The word comes from the use of showy and flamboyant vocabulary used by the 18th century English writer called Dr. Samuel Johnson (1709-84). He was a great dictator of language and his *A Dictionary of the English Language* (1755) as a lexicon is quite scholarly in scope and breadth. He was fond of difficult and showy language and this defined much of the rhetoric of the Neoclassical Period, also popularly known as the 18th century or the "Age of Prose and Reason." The next literary age, also called the Age of the Romantic Revival revolted against such a diction. This style became so pervasive that commentators labelled this as "Johnsonese", a style of writing characterized by him. Some of the examples are:

Here are some examples of Johnsonese in use:

- "The stuffed buckram of Johnsonese had been succeeded by the mincing hifalutin of Mrs. Anne Radcliffe and her like".
- "When he wrote for publication he did his sentences out of English into Johnsonese".
- "But Johnson seems to have written Johnsonese from his cradle"

As per *Dictionary.com,* some examples are: <u>JOHNSONESE Definition & Meaning | Dictionary.com</u>

a. His contrast between the simple, nervous and picturesque expression of Johnson's familiar letters and his Latinised pomposity when his sentences are done out of English into Johnsonese, cannot be forgotten; and his treatment of Bacon's style is as sound and excellent as his treatment of Bacon's philosophy is mistaken and false.

b. And if its author has certain qualities in common with his own "solemn elephant reposing in the shade," they are, one feels, the product of a character that, like Donne's elephant, could hardly be dislodged without the noise and cataclysm of a whole town undermined—whereas much of the style of to-day, which despises what it calls "Johnsonese," could be blown away with a puff of wind.

Imagine you have an expression like "flagrant conflagration". How many of you can comprehend it as meaning simply "wild fire." This is an instance of Johnsonese.

iii. Journalese:

This refers to certain kinds of journalistic writing that is typical with newspapers and journals. This means that the diction that is used is more of used in media. One example should suffice:

"Mother of five killed in a road accident."

This give us an impression that the person who perished was five years old! This is impossible as a five-year-old cannot be a mother. Hence, by means of an extended logic, we deduce that the lady killed had five children. There are many such examples that may confuse a potential reader.

E. The Structure of a Sentence

Proper comprehension of sentence structures is a vital skill for language proficiency. This means that you need to have a firm grasp of grammatical structures in English. English as a language follows the **S-V-O** pattern normally, which translates to subject-verb-object. Let's take an instance:

Ram eats a mango

He is a good boy

Most of these sentences adhere to this pattern. Thus, if we reverse the order of words, this will not yield any meaning:

Mango eats a Ram

Boy good he is

Thus, we come to the very vital point of syntax, or sentence structure. Syntactical errors are very common and can be a nuisance for a discerning reader. This can be due to the use of non-essential words like jargon, prepositions, jumbling of tenses and other factors. Often, translating verbatim from a source language to a target language under the MTI or Mother Tongue Influence and even vocabulary can be disturbing. Though there is no one rule that talks about an 'ideal' sentence structure, sentences can be written in a conversational tone and a lucid style.

F. How your sentence 'speaks'?

Sentences 'speak' for themselves. This means that how we frame our sentences talk volumes about our intentions as a communicator. This also, further, implies that sentences need to be framed in the right spirit. We need to keep the given points in mind:

i. Avoid using hackneyed vocabulary
ii. Use a conversational tone
iii. Avoid using jargon
iv. Keep technical words to a bare minimum
v. Use short sentences
vi. Keep an eye on the tenses and active-passive voice

Here are some examples of good sentences:

- "Hydrophobic plants hate water"
- "The meeting starts at 9 AM"
- "My grandmother is sick"
- "We had a really good time together"
- "There's nothing better than a good cup of hot coffee"
- "He was very good at his work"
- "I'm not very good at singing"
- "He is one of the best players in the world"

A good sentence is clear, concise, and leads the narrative forward. It also contains a subject, a verb, and an independent clause. An independent clause is a group of words that can stand alone as a complete sentence.

G. Videoconferencing and Communication

Videoconferencing has become a powerful means to connect with people all over the globe. We have people who now connect via various platforms like Google Meet, Zoom, Microsoft Teams and the like.

It becomes imperative on our part to use a language that is comprehensible and clear to people who are connecting with us thousands of kilometers away. Firstly, we should know that technology—internet connectivity is a major issue, that may snap at any point of time. Secondly, any ambiguous sentence or associated construction can break communication that is not happening face-to-face. This can be alarming. Some of the tips for better videoconferencing are, but not limited to:

- Ensure you have a stable internet connection
- Use unambiguous expressions
- Look cheerful
- Be attentive
- Be relaxed
- Use short sentences and a conversational tone.

Self-Assessment Questions

1. The remark that we sit under the shade of a tree that was planted by someone else highlights the need to:

    i. Have a team
    ii. The importance of group cohesion
    iii. The need to be selfish and forget the past contributions of others
    iv. None

2. Ergonomics is:

    i. A study of water harvesting technology
    ii. A study of workplace ambience
    iii. A study of the documentation process in formal settings
    iv. None

3. The definition of a team incorporates:

    i. Goals
    ii. Purposes
    iii. Hobbies
    iv. None

4. Teamwork is important to:

    i. Get things done
    ii. Be on the track

   iii. Meet deadlines

   iv. All

5. "Teamwork cannot proceed without a leader." The remark is:

   i. True

   ii. False

   iii. Both

   iv. Difficult to determine

Terminal Questions

1. Why do you need a toolkit for writing?

1. Explain Johnsonese and Journalese.

3. What do you mean by conditionals? Do you feel they are important in the negotiation of meaning and form part of the essential writing toolkit?

Self-Assessment Questions

Activity

Activity type: Offline Duration: 40 Minutes
  Description:
You are about to make your own Resume for a job. List 10 writing toolkits you might need.
  Video Links
  The Essential Writing Kit
  The ESSENTIAL Toolkit every Novel WRITER should have! - YouTube
  Essential Technical Writing Skills in 2022
  Essential Technical Writing Skills 2022- Youtube
  Introduction to Technical Writing
  Introduction to Technical Writing-Youtube
  End Notes:

Dictionary.Com. "Johnsonese: Definition and Meaning." JOHNSONESE Definition & Meaning | Dictionary.com. Accessed 10 May 2024.

BIBLIOGRAPHY

• 95 •

External Resources

Helden, L. G. (1971). *BasicEnglishSentencePatterns*. Educators Publishing Service.

Hornby, A. S. (1997). *Guide to Patterns and U age in English.* 2nd ed. Oxford University Press.

Wren, P. C., & Martin, H. (2007). *High School English Grammar & Composition.*

Rev. by N.D.V. Prasada Rao. New Delhi: S. Chand.

Keywords
Johnsonese
Journalese
Toolkit
Video conferencing

CHAPTER SEVEN

The Professional Context

You had the opportunity of knowing what the key soft skills are you need for the workplace. While doing so, you also might have noted that they operate in certain contexts— here, formal contexts. An intuitive understanding of what formal contexts are and under what conditions they operate was also specified. You, by now, might have an idea of how to use appropriate body language in formal settings. This unit deals with comprehension of documents and their types in formal settings. Though we already had a peek into what are those documents are, we will take stock of the idea of comprehension vis-à-vis such documents and how we make or should make sense of them. Reading is often the first step. Let's investigate the issues here.

A. **The question of comprehension**

The comprehension of texts in the professional sphere is a vital soft skill. Texts, whether they operate in formal or informal settings work in a special way. Texts are often, as the Soviet theorist Mikhail Bhaktin (1895-1975) says, "polyphonic"—a text in question has numerous viewpoints and voices jostling to grasp attention from the reader. Though this analysis of texts is more attuned for literary analysis, texts in the formal sphere also are fit for a polyphonic analysis. Suppose you're told to write a report after a presentation. You will not only put forth the data that was discussed in the meeting, the quantitative analysis of a certain aspect, but also spell your own viewpoints as to what to do with the data received to help the organization. Thus, anyone reading such a text as either an official document or for a 'polyphonic' analysis shall have to take into consideration two parallel discourses, the data per se and your own interpretation of the data. The text should be read in tandem with these two narrative strategies. Your interpretation of the data coupled with the data per se will lead to a competent analysis of the text.

As per *Frontiers in Psychology*, modern day textual comprehension calls for an analysis of multiple texts owing to the complexity of the digital era. To quote them:

The digital revolution has made a multitude of text documents from highly diverse perspectives on almost any topic easily available. Accordingly, the ability to integrate and evaluate information from different sources, known as multiple document comprehension, has become increasingly important. Because multiple document comprehension requires the integration of content and source information across texts, it is assumed to exceed the demands of single text comprehension due to the inclusion of two additional mental representations: the integrated situation model and the intertext model. [1]

It might be possible that you may have to comprehend multiple texts at the workplace. As an HR, you may have to read letters, memos, an email and even a policy document from the government. By now, you must have had the idea of how these are texts of a different kind with various narrative strategies—while an email is just meant to inform and even direct an employee to do something, policy documents have an air of finality within them and are written in a highly impersonal manner. Similarly, a piece of paper carrying some instructions from your boss is not composed as an email would be. So, what sets them apart? The register and the context. An email with a personal tone may have within itself an official undercurrent, while a policy document may read like a cautionary tale of sorts. If the government talks about the ban of plastic and gives anecdotes and examples to make it an interesting read, you might feel that you are not reading an official document, but something else.

How you differentiate between texts and respond to them is a key soft skill and it is still not clear as to how does the human brain make a clear demarcation between such a welter of competing data. The Oxford Historian Yuval Noah Harari in his book *Sapiens: A Brief History of Humankind* (2011) points out that this multi-tasking capacity of the brain still remains a mystery and is not well-understood yet. To quote him, the "brain's retrieval system is amazingly efficient, except when you are trying to remember where you put your car keys." [2]

B. Bottom-up and top-down reading

Reading and speaking are active skills. This does not mean that listening is not an active skill at all. In pervious units, you saw how listening is a soft skill that has to be mastered. But the question that has to be answered now is—how do we make sense of texts that we encounter daily? They are of various kinds and discourses that call for a melange of approaches to make sense of them. Suppose you have a newspaper with you and a letter from your wife living away to come to her rescue due to an emergency. Do you respond to both the texts in the same manner? Definitely not. The reasons could be many. But suppose that you come to know from a newspaper that the company you're working in will be merging with a bigger conglomerate that affects over three hundred employees, including you. And with that, an email or a whats app message arrives from your wife asking you to join relatives for the celebration of a birthday party. Again, the reaction to your wife's message would be different, even though the message comes from none other than your wife!

So, how do we make sense of texts? There are four ways of doing this, but there could be many competing strategies:

      a. Bottom-Up reading
      b. Top-Down reading
      c. Skimming
      d. Scanning

As per *Key Concepts in ELT*:

In accounts of foreign-language listening and reading, perceptual information is often described as 'bottom-up', while information provided by context is said to be 'top-down'. The terms have been borrowed from cognitive psychology, but derive originally from computer science, where they distinguish processes that are data-driven from those that are knowledge-driven.

Bottom-Up reading has to do with perceptual information, while Top-down is related to contextual information. Sounds big? It could be as these terms have been borrowed from computer science when it comes to data processing. As our brains are computers in themselves, they behave very much like machines. We are exposed to information; we establish an eye-contact with the words and take in the raw data and process it into meaningful information. This is the first step. The second important factor is the use of eye movements. To read properly and make a meaning of texts, your eyes need to be properly aligned to the words on paper. There could be instances wherein you may have to go back to a previous cluster of words and re-read a line or two again to make sense of the same.

As mentioned earlier, bottom-up reading is a kind of a textual strategy—it is just one of the many ways we make sense of texts and associated parameters. This happens when we read a text to get an idea of the words, phrases and the syntax as a whole. The question of eye movements come into effect during this kind of a reading strategy. A reader, during such a reading strategy makes use of his/her active as well as passive vocabulary to make sense of words that s/he does not comprehend. Also, there is a conscious effort on part of the reader to understand the sound system as a whole. If there is a difficult word or phrase, the reader tries to negotiate the meaning based on his/her own stock of vocabulary. Look at the group of sentences below:

"The man was inextricably bound to his own place and shuddered if he had to change the place he was nestled in. He was supposed to cook up a story to escape his predicament, but at such a mellow age, prevarication was something he was not wont to do."

As you can see, there are difficult words and phrases that the reader must negotiate. S/he might have to consult a dictionary or go online. If you cannot get hold of the words, you will have difficulty comprehending the *meaning* of the sentences. But even if you cross this step, you might have to a top-down reading. This involves understanding the context. Contextual parameters involve our schemata or background knowledge. Look at the set of sentences below adapted from the novel *Pride and Prejudice* (1813) by Jane Austen:

"It is a truth universally acknowledged, that a single man in possession of a good fortune, must be in want of a wife."

A comprehension of this passage has to take into account not only the readers' knowledge of what an 'ideal' marriage is, but also what it was supposed to be in the Romantic and early Victorian era in Britain where women were yet not easily entitled to property and inheritance rights. Thus, as per British Council, "Bottom-up processing happens when someone tries to understand language by looking at individual meanings or grammatical characteristics of the most basic units of the text, (e.g., sounds for a listening or words for a reading), and moves from these to trying to understand the whole text.

Self-Assessment Questions

1. Bottom-Up Reading has to do with:

   i.   Perceptual comprehension
   ii.   Contextual comprehension
   iii.   Both
   iv.   None

2.   Top-Down reading has to do with:

   i.   Perceptual comprehension
   ii.   Contextual comprehension
   iii.   Both
   iv.   None

3.   "Your eye movements can waver back and forth during reading--- this is a sign of a weak comprehension of the text." The given remark is:

   i.   Partly true
   ii.   Definitely true
   iii.   None
   iv.   Absolutely false

4.   Schemata refers to:

   i.   Background knowledge
   ii.   Conceptual parameters
   iii.   Both
   iv.   None

5.   Which one among the following talks about the polyphonic nature of texts?

   i.   Victor Shklovsky
   ii.   Mikhail Bakhtin
   iii.   T.S. Eliot
   iv.   Peter Widdowson

C. A Text in Question

You have already seen that texts can be of many kinds. The interpretation of a text calls for numerous strategies that are a melange of soft skills and prior schemata. In the foregoing paragraph, you also had a peek into how we make sense of texts through bottom-up and top-down reading strategies. Skimming a text refers to reading the same casually and locating information through our involvement with key words and other allied linguistic features. Scanning refers to reading the text in detail to locate a specific information. We both skim as well as scan read in our daily lives. As per Butte College:

Skimming and scanning are reading techniques that use rapid eye movement and keywords to move quickly through text for slightly different purposes. Skimming is reading rapidly in order to get a general overview of the material. Scanning is reading rapidly in order to find specific facts. While skimming tells you what general information is within a section, scanning helps you locate a particular fact.

Let us now have a look at a text from **Your Article Library:**

The arrangement of finance is not very much complicated in case of sole proprietorship and partnership firms as the business is done on a small scale and proprietors are able to provide funds without much difficulty. But financing involves many problems in the case of big business undertakings which are generally organised in the form of companies or corporations. Big business operations need large amount of capital which requires financial experts to raise and utilise the financial resources. These undertaking normally take the form of the companies, the problem of modern business finance is for all practical purposes the problem of corporate finance. Corporate finance may be defined as the business activity concerned with planning, raising, and administering of funds used in the business.

The problem and scope of corporate finance has been defined by the **Encyclopaedia of Social Sciences Vol. IV** in the following words: "Corporation finance deals with the financial problems of corporate enterprises." [3]

D. **The register**

What do you think could be the passage all about? As you have guessed rightly, it is on corporate funding and finance. But have you ever wondered how did you make sense of this? Why, for instance, is the text the one on this topic and not a part of a brochure detailing how companies are merged and the finances involved therein? Or not one that details the activities of a postman on duty?

This is where an intimate knowledge of register comes in. Register refers to the specialised language used in a context that calls for it. For example, if you're to write an apology letter on behalf of your company to an aggrieved client, your language and the choice of words will hover around the use of expressions like "we apologize" or "regret". It will not be confident in tone and descriptive but be more attuned to transact a plain dealing with the person in question. The register thus used here is that used in corporate communication. As mentioned before, there are certain set rules of giving information here. Supplying more information would result in information overload, less will leave the reader uninformed.

E. The Discourse

You'll often hear expressions like "the discourse of a saint", or "the tale generates a discourse of neglect and deprivation." By the word "discourse", you'll get an idea of the general feel, tone and viewpoint adopted within a passage or a text. It refers to the kind of language used, i.e., the register and how the passage responds to the larger concerns of culture specific to that discourse and the semiotic environment surrounding it.

What discourse does this passage generate? Is it about the idea of a carefree existence? Or one of gloom and melancholy in today's era? Your answer will be an instant no. And the reason for this is that you intuitively understand while reading this passage that the subject is that of corporate finance. How did you arrive at this conclusion? By closely examining the words, the context, and the style. It is written in a formal and lucid style and befits one used in official communication. Words like "company", "utilize" and "financing" gives us cues. It is not about the merging of two big business houses as the words specific to this occasion like "merge", "join", "units", "merger", etc. are nowhere to be found. It tells about the pesky idea of generating funds for corporate existence. This lookout for words is the first step towards what is known as discourse analysis that eventually takes in the socio-cultural context as well.

F. The Body Language

Consider a scenario. You've entered an interview room. No doubt, the scenario is taxing and stressful. There are ten people inside and all the eyes are on you. You are told to sit, but your legs rattle. Somehow you sit and rather slouch than be erect and on your guard. Your eyes waver here and there, and you start sweating. Your lips are parched, and you even go to the extent of licking them, though a glass of water has been arranged for you.

Do you think you'll end up getting the job? The definite answer is a big NO. Why? Maybe, you'll say that you answered all the questions. But your level of confidence was not up to the mark. You displayed signs of nervousness and even fatigue which prevented you from getting the job. Having said that, your body language was not correct and showed signs of low confidence.

i. **How your body 'speaks': Issues at work**

Body language and paralanguage are two of the non-verbal skills. By verbal, we mean spoken skills, that is the art of correct and persuasive speaking or rhetoric. By non-verbal skills, we mean those features of our communication that help us communicate without words per se. Paralanguage is one part of this that refers to the tone, pitch, and intonation of our speech system. The other consists of body language. When you wave your hands without saying "good- bye", you are using your hands to communicate. Similarly, a nod by head signifies either a "yes" or a "no". See the images below and matters will be easier for you to follow:

Essential Body Language From: <8 Essential Body Language Tips for Radiating Confidence/Google>

As per the blog *Shipping Solutions*, "[b]ody language refers to facial expressions, gestures, position, and movement and their relation to communication. They differ greatly from culture to culture, and there is no dictionary to translate them." [5]

A positive body language is bound to leave a positive impression on others. There are soft skill experts who train students as to how they should use their body while communicating. This brings us to some more parameters in the discussion of body language. As mentioned, since the use of body language is a component of non-verbal communication, it often takes these forms:

i. Haptics
ii. Vocalics
iii. Chronemics
iv. Proxemics
v. Oculesics

Suppose you're sad and pent up. There is no one to console you. Suddenly, one of your friends comes and puts his/her hand on your shoulder. Though s/he does not speak, it conveys a lot. This is called **haptics**, how touch conveys message and the way it is encoded and decoded. The same touch on a woman's shoulder from a male in a bus would invite a rude slap!

Vocalics refers to the use of your voice and its modulations to convey vital information. In the same vein, **chronemics** is the study of how an acute awareness of time is an indicator of messages. Consider a scenario where your boss has convened as meeting at 3 PM but no one enters the room before 3:30. Your boss acquires a different body language and might look pissed and angry—a natural consequence when no one adheres to his instructions.

Proxemics is the study of how the sense of space transmits vital information. If a man, a complete stranger moves very close to a woman, the latter would definitely mind the move; on the other hand, one's spouse would not. **Oculesics** is the study of how eye-contact conveys messages. If you stare at a girl, she will feel offended, but a decent eye contact would not be an issue.

G. Video-conferencing and communication

Videoconferencing and Communication: A Revolution in How We Connect

In the modern world, communication is key to success in personal, educational, and professional life. With the advent of technology, traditional forms of communication, such as face-to-face interactions and written correspondence, have evolved to meet the demands of a more connected and fast-paced society. One of the most significant developments in this transformation has been the rise of videoconferencing. Videoconferencing enables people to connect in real-time, face-to-face, regardless of geographical distance, thus redefining the way we communicate. This essay explores how videoconferencing has revolutionized communication, examining its advantages, challenges, and its role in various fields.

The Evolution of Communication

Historically, communication was limited by physical barriers. The invention of the telephone in the late 19th century was a significant breakthrough, allowing people to communicate over long distances through voice. However, it was still limited to one sense—sound. Over time, other communication technologies emerged, including television, radio, and, eventually, the internet, which paved the way for modern-day videoconferencing. The introduction of high-speed internet and the development of software applications such as Zoom, Microsoft Teams, and Skype have made videoconferencing a common and integral part of daily life for millions of people worldwide.

Videoconferencing combines both video and audio, allowing users to communicate visually and verbally. This technological advancement creates an immersive communication experience that closely mimics face-to-face interactions, allowing for greater understanding through body language, facial expressions, and tone of voice.

Advantages of Videoconferencing

1. **Breaking Geographical Barriers**: One of the most compelling advantages of videoconferencing is its ability to connect people across vast distances. In the past, international meetings or collaborations required significant travel time and expense. Today, videoconferencing allows individuals to participate in real-time discussions from anywhere in the world. Whether it's for business meetings, academic collaborations, or personal connections, geographical location is no longer a limitation.

2. **Cost and Time Efficiency**: Travel costs can be a major burden for businesses, educational institutions, and individuals. With videoconferencing, organizations save money by reducing the need for business trips, flights, and accommodation expenses. Additionally, the time saved from travel allows people to allocate their time more effectively, focusing on work or other activities.

3. **Increased Collaboration**: In business, education, and other fields, effective collaboration is essential. Videoconferencing provides an environment where people can share documents, presentations, and ideas instantly. Collaborative tools such as screen sharing and virtual whiteboards enhance teamwork, making it easier for participants to interact and brainstorm in real time. This level of collaboration strengthens the decision-making process and fosters innovation.

4. **Flexibility and Accessibility**: Videoconferencing also promotes flexibility, as participants can join meetings from their homes or offices, eliminating the need for physical presence. This accessibility is especially valuable for people with disabilities, as it allows them to participate in discussions without the need for extensive travel. Furthermore, the flexibility of videoconferencing can accommodate different time zones, enabling businesses and institutions to work globally without the constraints of standard office hours.

Challenges of Videoconferencing

Despite its many benefits, videoconferencing is not without its challenges. Some of the most common issues that arise include:

1. **Technical Difficulties**: Videoconferencing relies on a stable internet connection, and any disruptions to this connection—such as poor internet speed or hardware malfunctions—can hinder communication. Problems with video or audio quality can also lead to misunderstandings or missed information, making the conversation less effective.

2. **Lack of Non-Verbal Cues**: While videoconferencing provides visual communication, it is still not a perfect substitute for in-person interactions. The lack of full sensory engagement can lead to misinterpretations of tone or body language. Small nuances such as posture or gestures may be lost, which can impact the depth of the conversation and the building of rapport.

3. **Privacy and Security Concerns**: As videoconferencing becomes more widely used, the issue of privacy and data security has come to the forefront. Cyberattacks, hacking, and unauthorized access to video calls can compromise sensitive information. To ensure secure communication, users must adopt best practices, such as using encrypted platforms, setting up strong passwords, and avoiding sharing personal details over unsecured networks.

4. **Over-reliance on Technology**: While videoconferencing has become an essential tool for communication, over-reliance on it can reduce face-to-face interaction, which is important for building stronger relationships and fostering empathy. Constant screen time can also lead to burnout and diminish the quality of personal communication.

The Role of Videoconferencing in Various Fields

1. **Business and Work**: In the business world, videoconferencing has become a key tool for remote work, allowing teams to collaborate seamlessly across locations. It enables virtual meetings, presentations, and interviews, making it an essential tool in the modern workplace. The COVID-19 pandemic accelerated the adoption of remote work and videoconferencing, solidifying its importance for business continuity and employee well-being.
2. **Education**: Videoconferencing has transformed education, particularly with the rise of online learning. Students can attend classes virtually, participate in group discussions, and even take exams remotely. Teachers and students can engage in real-time interactions, providing a dynamic learning experience. Educational institutions have also used videoconferencing for guest lectures, virtual tours, and international exchanges, expanding students' horizons beyond their local communities.
3. **Healthcare**: Telemedicine is another sector where videoconferencing has proven invaluable. Patients can consult with doctors remotely, receive diagnoses, and even follow up on treatments without having to leave their homes. This is particularly beneficial for individuals living in rural or remote areas, where access to healthcare services may be limited. Furthermore, during health crises like the COVID-19 pandemic, videoconferencing allowed healthcare providers to continue consultations while minimizing the risk of infection.
4. **Social and Personal Connections**: Beyond the professional and academic uses, videoconferencing has strengthened personal relationships. Family members and friends separated by distance can stay connected, share moments, and maintain emotional bonds. Videoconferencing platforms also enable virtual events such as weddings, birthdays, and celebrations, providing a means for loved ones to come together despite physical separation.

The first conceptualisation of image transfer emerged along with the development of wire-delivered audio in the 1870s, but the first formal attempts at videoconferencing began in the United States in the 1920s. In 1927 Bell Labs connected Secretary of Commerce Herbert Hoover and other officials in Washington, D.C., with AT&T President Walter Gifford in New York City; the two-way audio connection was accompanied by a one- way video connection from Washington. D.C., to New York. Experimentation continued during the 1930s in Europe, where television technologies were more mature. By 1964, AT&T was ready to introduce its first public videoconferencing tool—a videophone called the Picturephone.

Whatever be the history of videoconferencing, the rules of the 'game' remain the same. Proper body language must be maintained and a clarity in speech, a much sought-after attribute in online meetings is a recommended element. Videoconferencing is only possible due to a stable internet connection and clarity of voice is a must.

Self-Assessment Questions

6. Body language refers to the way you communicate non-verbally. The remark is:

    i.   True
    ii. False
    iii. Cannot be determined
    iv. Both true as well as false.

7. The manner you communicate through touch is called:

    i.   Haptics
    ii. Chronemics
    iii. Oculesics
    iv. Proxemics

8. Telespace is:

    i.   A videoconferencing platform
    ii. A social media site
    iii. An e-commerce site
    iv. A reading app like Kindle

9. The first conceptualisation of image transfer was in the:

    i.   1990s
   ii.   1870s
  iii.   1970s
   iv.   1900s

10. AT&T launched the first videoconferencing tool called:

    i.   Picture phone
   ii.   Video phone
  iii.   TeleX Phone
   iv.   Skype

H. **Work Etiquette**

Let's discuss one more topic that is in consonance with formal settings and the manner you should carry yourself in such situations. This has to do with work etiquette. Can you tell what does this mean? It just implies the basic fact that there are certain implied as well as explicit rules while working in a formal setting. This undoubtedly differs from the manner in which you're supposed to behave in informal settings with your pals and family. Let us see the rules of the 'game' now.

i. **The situation**

A 'situation' in a formal context means not only the context, but also the register that we are supposed to use and the communicative strategy we are to adopt. It is important to keep in mind this situation, as the same gives us an idea of the feel for the 'game'. Game here refers to the game of power relations, one of the cardinal factors in the communicative context. Suppose you're attending a meeting where you have to put forth your viewpoints regarding a matter that has cropped up. You dress nicely and jot down the major points to be discussed. But when you join the meeting, you're sidelined and not given much room to air your opinions. What is at fault? Your attire? Your communication? No. It is not about you. It is about the power politics at work. If your boss keeps speaking all the time, there is little reason for you to communicate. This is not your fault. It is the shortcoming posed by the 'situation' or the context.

ii. **The semiotic system**

Let's probe the same matter a bit deeper. Work etiquette is influenced not only by the power relations but also by your own intuitive understanding of the semiotic system. Sounds big? A semiotic system refers to a particular sign system. The Swiss linguist Ferdinand de Saussure (1857-1913) laid the foundation of semiotics in language study and the same has been extended to fields as diverse as literary and cultural studies, anthropology, gender studies and the like. As per this theory of signs, the entire world around us is a complex sign system. When the traffic lights go green, you're supposed to cross the road, when they are red, you know you have to wait. How do you know this? Does a policeman on the road shout and tell you to stop? Not at all. The red signal means you must stop, and the green implies that you need to move ahead. This is the sign system.

Thus, an understanding of the context or the sign system in which you work is important. Work etiquette is this inherent feel for the sign system at workplace. Work etiquette is a huge area and a topic fit for critical analysis, but for the sake of your understanding, do note the following:

a. **Be on time**. This is one of the hallmarks of proper work etiquette.
b. **Be courteous** to members of the opposite gender. Care for their suggestions.
c. **Do not bicker** on petty matters. This lowers your estimation in the eyes of others.
d. **Dress well** and maintain proper hygiene.
e. **Be brief** and to the point. No one likes a talkative co-worker.
f. **Delegate your job** properly and try to maintain deadlines.
g. **Fulfil the expectations** of your organisation and earn rewards.
h. **Listen to the other side** and give ample room for your views as well.
a. **Avoid talking about private matters** and mixing personal issues with professional matters.
j. **Refrain from participating in groupthink** and put forth your honest suggestions.

Self-Assessment Questions

11. The phenomenon of going with the opinions of the larger group and not with what is impartial and correct is called:-

    i.   Herd think
    ii. People think iii.Groupthink iv. None

12. The field of semiotics deals with:

    i.   The sign system
    ii. Cultural factors
    iii. The context
    iv. All

13. A knowledge of workplace etiquette is important as:

    i.   It helps one sustain in the job
    ii. It helps one understand the overall job scenario
    iii. It helps one gain confidence in the job
    iv. All

14. The study of semiotics was first advocated by:

    i.   Ferdinand de Saussure
    ii. Noam Chomsky
    iii. Dell Hymes
    iv. MAK Halliday

15. "Power dynamics is an integral part of the workplace scenario." The given remark is:

    i.   Always true
    ii. Sometimes true
    iii. False
    iv. Both always true as well as false

Summary

Team building and work etiquette are key soft skills. A team is needed to gain cohesion and perform better, thereby meeting deadlines in an effective way.

The ambience at workplace is important as well. Ergonomics is the study of ambience at workplace. A crowded workplace is bound to hamper productivity.

One should have a knowledge of the working environment at work. This refers to the sign system and an intuitive comprehension of the power games that people play on each other.

Body language is a non-verbal strategy to get a message across. It can be divided into chronemics, oculesics, haptics, vocalics and proxemics.

There are certain set rules or work etiquette while working in a formal setting. This involves a few factors like speaking, documenting, and behaving in the prescribed manner as stipulated.

Terminal Questions

1. What do you mean by a team? Why is cohesion important for a team?

2. What do you mean by body language? Why is it important? Discuss.

3. What is understood by the term haptics and chronemics? Provide some examples.

Activity
Activity type: Offline Duration: 40 Minutes
Description:
Mr. X has joined a new firm. He is enthusiastic to meet his team and, to that end, ends up going into every body's console or chamber, thereby interrupting their work. He is not too conscious of the basic fact that a minimum of physical distance ought to be maintained between two parties talking. He is, thus, ignored by most people despite being energetic and dynamic.

What possible solution can you suggest for him? Note them down and involve your co-learner into this process. One has been done for you.

a. Suggest a soft skills training course for him.

b.

c.

d.

End Notes

1.   *Frontiers in Psychology.* "More Than (Single)-text comprehension?—On University Students' Comprehension of Multiple Documents".

https://www.frontiersin.org/articles/10.3389/fpsyg.2020.562450/full. Accessed 10 June 2024.

2. Nuval Noah Harari. *A Brief History of Humankind.* Random House, 2011.

3. Edwin Robert Anderson Seligman, and Alvin Saunders Johnson. *Encyclopedia of Social Sciences.* Vol. 4. MacMillan, 1931.

BIBLIOGRAPHY

External Resources

Goetsch, D. L., & Kalia, S. (2018). *Effective Teamwork.* Pearson.

Mitra, B. K. (2006). *Effective Technical Communication: Guide for Scientists and Engineers.* OUP India.

Pease, B. (2006). *The Definitive Book of Body Language: The Hidden Meaning Behind People's Gestures and Expressions.* RHUS.

Video links

Topic

Link

Teamwork and cohesion

https://www.youtube.com/watch?v=O4yBPMpBZM4

Body Language

https://www.youtube.com/watch?v=4jwUXV4QaTwhttps://www.youtube.com/watch?v=MmN_W7ncL2I

https://www.youtube.com/watch?v=1sfM-xx7tHI

Workplace Etiquette

https://www.youtube.com/watch?v=_6Cz4kKG23s

Ambience at Workplace

https://www.youtube.com/watch?v=PYJ22-YYNW8https://www.youtube.com/watch?v=f3ds-7-EU00

Keywords

Team building Time management

Workplace communication Soft skills

Communicative strategy

CHAPTER EIGHT

Paperwork and You

Documentation is the backbone of any well-functioning organization. Whether it is used for recording processes, tracking decisions, or preserving institutional knowledge, documentation serves as a critical tool to ensure efficiency, continuity, and accountability in the workplace. Despite its significance, documentation is often overlooked or poorly managed, leading to inefficiencies, miscommunication, and operational risks. This essay explores the importance of documentation in the workplace, the challenges associated with it, and best practices for creating and maintaining effective documentation.

In its simplest form, documentation refers to the process of recording information in a structured manner for future reference. This can include written records, digital files, or multimedia formats that capture details about projects, processes, policies, and other organizational activities. Examples of workplace documentation include standard operating procedures (SOPs), meeting minutes, project plans, employee handbooks, training materials, and financial records.

Organizations often face turnover as employees move on to new opportunities or retire. Without proper documentation, the knowledge these employees possess may leave with them, creating gaps in organizational memory. Documenting processes, procedures, and project histories ensures that critical information is preserved and accessible to current and future employees.

Clear and well-maintained documentation eliminates ambiguity and provides employees with a reliable resource to perform tasks accurately. Standard operating procedures, for instance, ensure consistency in how tasks are executed, reducing the likelihood of errors and increasing overall efficiency. This is particularly important in industries such as healthcare, manufacturing, and technology, where precision is crucial.

Comprehensive documentation is a valuable asset for onboarding new employees and training existing staff. New hires can refer to employee handbooks, job aids, and process guides to familiarize themselves with their roles and responsibilities. Similarly, training materials can help employees acquire new skills and adapt to changes in the workplace.

Many industries are subject to stringent regulatory requirements. Proper documentation helps organizations demonstrate compliance with laws, standards, and industry best practices. For example, in finance and healthcare, maintaining accurate records is essential to avoid legal repercussions and financial penalties. Additionally, documentation provides a paper trail that can be used to address disputes or conduct audits.

Documentation serves as a reference point for team members, facilitating clear communication and reducing misunderstandings. For instance, project documentation ensures that everyone involved is aligned on objectives, timelines, and deliverables. This is especially critical for remote or distributed teams, where face-to-face interactions are limited.

Accurate and up-to-date documentation provides managers and stakeholders with the information they need to make informed decisions. Whether it involves analyzing past performance, forecasting future trends, or planning strategic initiatives, documentation serves as a reliable source of data and insights.

We saw the nature of workplace documentation. Workplace communication operates within a particular context and that there are set rules that you are expected to follow in such a scenario. You also came to know that for effective transaction of day- to-day activities in the formal context, an intimate knowledge of discourse and power relations is a must. As a matter of common sense, such communications can take the form of both verbal as well as written communications.

Here, we'll focus on how communication takes place and concomitant communicative strategies are framed within an organisation. However, it is necessary to know the various ways in which information flow operates within an organisation.

A. **Internal correspondence**

By internal correspondence, we mean the multifarious ways in which communication is directed within an organisation. While working, you'll probably see that you're supposed to communicate with various departments within the institution you're working in. You may be told to comply with an order or be asked to issue one.

Consider a scenario where a message was supposed to pass from desk A of a government organisation to desk F. Now, there are multiple desks in between. A message transmits some information and is subject to misinterpretation on account of myriad factors like the channel, the receiver, the cultural predilections of the sender or receiver and even the nature of the message. Suppose the initial message was: "There is a possibility of extending a week's summer vacation to the new members in our organisation, though there has been no official information. The same is awaited." Now, when this message passes through various desks or "workstations", the possibility of the message getting distorted becomes high as the chances of misinterpretation is on the higher side as well. It may be possible that the person on desk D is new to the organisation, and s/he reacts to the same in a positive or even jubilant mood. The same now becomes:

"One week's vacation is extended to the new faculties in the organisation, the official notification is awaited."

See the difference! The message that was intended to convey a particular information ended up conveying something else. This is what happens when a message passes through different layers or hierarchies. This may end up distorting the message and conjuring a disconcerting picture of what is not.

As per *Forbes*, internal communication may suffer from a good number of setbacks:

Poor communication is a constant problem in companies. You can have three diligent people all working to get something done, and all operating on completely different interpretations of what that task is supposed to be. Team leads can miss internal memos about problems or updates, and staff can become frustrated by vague or contradictory messages coming from different sections of the department. [1]

So how do you fix it? With a small team, you can get people into the same room to hash things out, but that's not always feasible, especially for larger groups. You need a process to consistently get good information out there so that people can immediately act.

Internal Communication can take many forms within an organisation. Let us see what those are:

i. Upward communication:

Upward communication refers to a situation when the communication within an organisation travels from the grassroots level to the topmost level. Take for instance a situation where there is a request from all the employees in your institution to extend the summer break from a week to a fortnight owing to severe heat wave. An application is sent to the CEO. This is an instance of upward communication. Both upward as well as downward communication are instances of vertical communication.

ii. Downward Communication:

Consider the other situation. Suppose that the CEO of the same company takes stock of the situation and sends a circular that the extension of the summer break is granted. In this case, communication flows from top to bottom — this is an example of downward communication.

iii. Horizontal communication:

This kind of communication takes place when communication happens among people of roughly the same rank. Take for instance that you're the Dean of Faculty Affairs in a university and you've called the Dean of International Outreach for clarification. In this case, since both the parties are more or less of the same rank, the type of communication here is horizontal communication.

iv. Grapevine communication:

Have you ever heard of rumours? Rumours are stories that may be true or false. Rumours are normal at a workplace, and you'd also find rumourmongers who love gossiping and spreading stories. Suppose you hear a story that one of the old and valued members of an organisation got fired. You try to verify the veracity of the statement and come to know that the same is false. This is what is called a rumour. This rumour-based, unofficial channel of communication that circulates in an otherwise official set up is called Grapevine communication. It is called so because the same resembles the vine of a grape bunch without any defining center and spreading in all directions.

B. External correspondence

Any organisation, if it wishes to thrive, must also concentrate on external correspondence. In a globalized era of today, there is no room for a closed existence. Companies are merged with other business houses and regular follow-up is done to ensure quality control. Though emails are the preferred way of sending messages, many companies still rely on business letters for transacting an affair. Such letters, printed on the official letter pads of an organisation include letters of inquiry, order, complaint and the like. Suppose you are working in a company that maintains a small library. Your organisation needs some books. You have located a publisher and written to them on behalf of your company to supply you with ten copies of a self- improvement book called *You Can Win* by Shiv Khera. You are supposed to write an order letter that may have a format like this:

Sample Order Letter

Manny Manufacturing, Inc. 4378 E. # 4th Street Place, Zip Code
February 5th, 2008 XYZ, Inc
Place, Zip Code
Attention: Sales Department
I'd like to order (mention the orders in a table). The reference numbers are from your 2003 catalogue. Please include a catalogue with my order.

I want this order to ship COD complete. If you cannot send the complete order within 10 days, please inform me immediately. I can be contacted at 87609967.

Thank you Name Designation
Self-Assessment Questions

1. Diagonal communication happens when:

    i.   When communication takes place by bypassing hierarchies
    ii. When communication takes place when it is directed upwards
    iii. When communication takes place when it is directed downwards
    iv. None

2. A boss sends a letter to his subordinates. This is an instance of:

    i.   Downward communication
    ii. Upward communication
    iii. Both
    iv. None

3. A worker sends an application to his boss for a pay hike. This is an instance of:

   i. Downward communication
   ii. Upward communication
   iii. Both
   iv. None

4. Downward communication is vertically aligned. This is:

   i. True
   ii. False
   iii. Cannot be determined
   iv. Both true as well as false

5. Grapevine communication is------------ in nature.

   i. Formal
   ii. Informal
   iii. Both partly
   iv. The question needs a review.

D. Emails

Emails are considered the most inexpensive and fastest way of sending messages. Though facing some serious competition from *WhatsApp* and *Telegram*, emails are still considered the accepted 'official' means to send messages to business clients and other stakeholders. You may message a person via *WhatsApp*, but it is not an official and formal way to send communication. Emails are reliable as they can be easily printed and produced as evidence.

The First Email, A Story!!

The history of email is interesting. As per the popular blog *Book Your Data* that provides interesting information about the humble origins of the emailing system:

The earliest email was very similar to simply leaving a note on someone's desk. At first, an email was simply a message that was placed in another user's file directory, in an area where they would be able to see it when they logged in. The first email system of this kind was the one used at the Massachusetts Institute of Technology in 1965. The system was known as MAILBOX. Another similar program that was used at the time to send messages was referred to as SNDMSG.

During the early era of email, mainframe computers could have up to one hundred users that would access the mainframe from their desks. As terminals connected to the mainframe were not equipped with memory or storage, all of the work was actually done on the remote mainframe computer. Because of this, prior to the invention of the internet, email could only be used to send messages to someone on the same mainframe computer. Today, experienced marketers are using prospecting tools like Bookyourdata [sic.] to buy email list.

Eventually, computers evolved and were able to communicate with each other over networks. This caused the email system to become a bit more complex as now a specific address needed to be indicated so that electronic messages got to the correct address. A man by the name of Ray Tomlinson is actually credited with inventing the modern email system that we know today. In 1972, while working as an ARPANET contractor for Bolt Beranek and Newman, Tomlinson chose to use the @ symbol to denote the sending of messages from one computer to another computer.

Obviously, sending emails was made possible due to the Internet. A forerunner to the Internet or the World Wide Web was the ARPANET, that stood for Advanced Research Projects Agency Network, established by the US Defence in 1969. It was discontinued in the early 1990s after the advent of the "www".

i. **Proper email etiquette**

Any formal communication, as we have seen in the foregoing units, has to confirm to the register and the communicative scenario. A proper email can have a positive impact on the audience, while a negative one can ruin one's job prospects and career. Let's now have a look at some of the ways in which an email message can have its desired effect.

a. Always use the subject line judiciously. The subject line should clearly mention the motive behind sending an email.
b. Be careful to note if the mail you're sending is suited for the formal or informal scenario. There would obviously be a

huge difference between the email sent to your boss asking for a favour and your pal enquiring how the last trip went.

c. Writing the email in capitals letters throughout is like shouting to the other person. Never do that.

d. The act of replying to all is to be resorted to only when it is neede There is no point clogging the other party's mailbox with messages not relevant to them.

e. Mention your name in full and that of your organisation while sending an official email. An appropriate closing remark is a bonus.

f. Go for a spelling check and use tools like *Grammarly* to proof-read.

Self-Assessment Questions

6. "Writing emails in capitals, at least in some cases is needed, but writing so throughout is not advisable." The remark is:

  i. True
  ii. False
  iii. Both
  iv. Cannot be determined

7. The first email sent from space was in the year:

  i. 1998
  ii. 1991
  iii. 2000
  iv. 2002

8. Which of the following is vital in an email conversation?

  i. The overall language
  ii. An acute awareness of the context and register
  iii. Closing remarks
  iv. All

9. One of the tools widely used for proofreading texts is:

    i.   Grammarly
    ii. Petey
    iii. Mind Your Language!
    iv. All

10. ARPANET was initiated in the year:

    i.   1968
    ii. 1969
    iii. 1999
    iv. 1971

Case study

Mr. S works in an organisation that deals with supplying key hardware parts for oil drilling platforms. A machinery is needed by another company, and it has been reported to Mr. S via an email. Mr. S responds after a full 10 days:

From: cdp.1213@outlook.com   To: mary.cc@rocketmail.com   Cc: dmk.2021@gmail.com

All Mails 423

Spam 122

Trash 00 Bcc:

Re: Hi!!

Dear there!

Was offline. We'll get in touch with you regarding the query.

best

Mr. S

Operations.

[sent from iphone A50] [...]

----- Can you tell what is terribly wrong with this official email conversation? Hope you've guessed

it right. Now see the same email resent:

To: smith.cc@rocketmail.com

Cc: dmk.2021@gmail.com All Mails 423

Spam 122
Trash 00 Bcc:
Re: Your query for crawlers for your platform dtd. 05/23/2021
Dear Mr. Smith.

My apologies for not writing to you before. Due to scheduled maintenance work, most of us were compelled to go offline. I've passed your request to the department concerned. I am sure by now, your request has been accepted and you'll get a confirmation from our side within two business days.

Please get in touch for more queries and I'd be happy to help.
best
Mr. S
Head, Operations
BL Logistics Ltd. [A UK Govt. Undertaking] 10 Russell Street,
Norwich
The United Kingdom
PE29JX
Phone: +1-568974568
Ext: 012
www.bllogistics.com

You can see for yourself that the email has all the required features to have a positive impact on a client. It has a proper subject line, salutation and ending with complete address of the company along with its logo.

Self-Assessment Questions

11. What is evident from the case study above?

   i. That formal emails are to be drafted with care and caution
   ii. That we should not think much before sending emails
   iii. That the purpose of an email conversation should be stated clearly
   iv. Both (i) and (iii).

12. The email resent again is better than the one sent earlier as:

   i. The language has been taken care of
   ii. There is an inclusion of graphics and pictures

iii.   The email has weblinks
iv.   None

13.   The second email has the address of the company as well as its logo. This practice is:

i.   Necessary
ii.   Desirable but not necessary
iii.   Not at all necessary
iv.   None

14.   The 1ˢᵗ email uses no capital letters in the body of the email, and yet the same is not recommended in an official setting as:

i.   Due to utter disregard for the official nature of the communication process
ii.   Due to the flippant nature of the communicative event
iii.   Both
iv.   None

15.   The parting line in the 2ⁿᵈ email is important as:

i.   It shows the sender's genuine interest in the sender
ii.   It is a matter of courtesy and good manners
iii.   Both
iv.   None

C. **The Nature of External Communication**

We saw the complexities inherent in internal communication. You had the opportunity to take stock of how internal communication moves in a particular fashion with reference to the hierarchy in a professional setting. You could well discern how communication can either have a downward, upward or even an informal flow like the grapevine which is a marked feature of any formal setting. Though much of the communication nowadays happens through electronic means, you'd be surprised to know that written communication in the form of letters is still a welcome part of the same and even encouraged.

D. **Letter writing in a digital age**

As just mentioned, written communication is still a marked feature of the professional communication setup and even encouraged. You are sure to have come across written notices and circulars in your school and college days. This is also the case with respect to large multinational corporations and houses. You might be wondering here as to why would such organisations still resort to offline, written communication when the buzzword everywhere is to go "paperless." Going paperless is a good measure in an era of deforestation and dwindling natural resources, but online communication suffers from shortcomings as diverse as hacking and the propensity of the message being corrupted due to the online environment and the cyberspace at large. The internet is marked by its ever-changing and dynamic nature and a message might get corrupted. Drives may be unavailable at the time when the data is most needed for official purposes. Moreover, offline, written documents do not need a specialist hand to be sorted, while fishing out a message like an email sent around, say, a year ago might call into abilities like searching the mailbox or sorting in an expert manner with reference to key terms. As per *Forbes* in the article "Go Write a Letter: Ink and Paper in the Digital Age":

Imagine receiving a handwritten letter addressed to you from the CEO of your company. That letter would not need to be a Ph.D. thesis. A few sentences from the CEO, a director or a manager expressing that they saw you working hard on a project that is important and that they appreciated your dedication would have a tangible impact. [2]

Receiving words of gratitude on paper instead of email can have two effects: You likely feel a valuable part of the company and become an even more committed team member, and you're also much more likely to share that letter with your closest friends and loved ones. Quite honestly, people rarely frame emails; they frame letters.

Vancouver Manufacturing

9102 NW 99th Street, Vancouver, Washington 95665 (800) 555-1212

- www.example.com

September 25, 2005

Mr. John Taylor Director of Operations ABC Corporation

100 E Main Street Vancouver, WA 98685

Dear Mr. Taylor:

As our new letterhead indicates, we have recently changed the name of our business from Fort Vancouver Manufacturing to Vancouver Manufacturing.

There has been no change in management and we will be providing the same products and fine service on which we have built our reputation in the industry. We would appreciate it if you would bring this announcement to the attention of your accounts payable department and direct them accordingly.

Thank you for being one of our valued customers. We appreciate your cooperation in this matter.

Al Olsen

President, Vancouver Manufacturing

An Official Letter

The key documents that can be sent either online or offline outside an organisation include letters of appreciation, recommendation, complaint, orders, supplies and the like. There could be many more, depending on the situation—you'd also have legal letters and notices sent on behalf of an organisation to a client for non-payment of dues for instance. Suppose an organisation is looking for a security guard. It would search the web and come across a security services supplier. The organisation may send a letter to the same asking for the credentials of a Mr. XYZ and the security services company may revert back in a similar fashion, sending a hardcopy of a letter that was also emailed. It may recommend the man in question, highlighting the commendable qualities in him. This is known as a recommendation letter.

Similarly, suppose you're working as a librarian of a college. Various departments have sent requisitions for books and you're supposed to take care of the matter. You send an order letter to a renowned publishing company and distributors to supply the needed books along with the number of copies and other specifications. This is called an order letter. If, after getting the orders, you notice that some of the books are not up to the quality and the consignment arrived in a pretty bad state, you are supposed to send a complaint letter. Documents sent to a client for non-payment of dues are often legal in nature and are known as settlement documents. However, they should be sent as a last resort.

E. Looking for a job

Have you ever heard of the phrase "job hunting"? Well, it is one that many of us hate. After getting your degree, you will have to look for a job. This is something that will inevitably land to your lot. Unless you have campus placements in good companies by top notch engineering colleges, you'll have to fend for yourself. Scary and intense? This is as bad as it can get. So, how to bypass this situation? The standard procedure for this is to write job applications to prospective employers, along with a resume or a CV. And there should also be a cover letter. We'll discuss CV and resume writing in the next sub-unit. Let us now investigate the mechanics of writing a cover letter, which is one of the aspects of external communication. It is external in nature as it is sent from a sender looking for a job to someone stationed within an institution. It is 'external' as it travels distances, whether as a letter or 'snail-mail', or as an email.

Now that you've got some idea of what a cover letter is, let us see why it is important and how you

can draft an effective cover letter. As per Michael Page, a cover letter is important as:

A cover letter accompanies your CV as part of most job applications. It provides the hiring manager with further detail on how your skill set aligns with the role, what you can bring to the team and why you want the position. Cover letters also allow the recruiter and hiring manager to develop a better understanding of your suitability for a position. [3]

Your cover letter will often make the first impression in the mind of a hiring manager, making it an essential part of your application. In addition to this, employers tend to favour CVs that are accompanied by a cover letter and will often specifically request one as a mandatory requirement to apply for their vacancies.

A cover letter is important as:

a. It **provides vital information** about your profile in a nutshell that is covered in greater detail by your CV or resume.

b. Cover letters are **an apt prelude to the CV or resume** and are normally placed at the top.

c. It is a kind of an **introduction to your CV** or resume.

Since a cover letter employs a somewhat conversational tone, it is **often preferred by employers** who have little time to read your CVs or resumes.

Cover letters or any official letter nowadays is written in what is called the **full block layout**. This is a neat layout wherein everything is fully flushed towards the left side, even the date and closing remarks. This gives a clean impression of your writing style. Another layout style is the **modified**

block layout that is slowly becoming obsolete.

Below is a sample cover letter in a full block layout format for a job. It is also called a job application:

SAMPLE INTERNSHIP APPLICATION LETTER

543 Willow Drive Terre Haute,

IN 47802 812-555-7777

March 19, 2009

Mr. John Miller

Data Processing Manager

Industrial Outlet Corporation

293 Corporate Square

Terre Haute,

IN 47803

Dear Mr. Miller:

Please consider me for the Information System Administrator Internship that was listed with the Indiana State University Career Center. This internship is of great interest to me as it reflects my career goals and requires my education, skills, and experience.

With majors in mathematics and computer science, I have extensive knowledge of database design and computer programming. In addition, elective courses in finance have provided knowledge of forecasting, evaluating ratios, and analyzing complex and detailed financial information. Moreover, working as a Student Assistant in the IT Lab at Indiana State University developed my ability to communicate ideas clearly and enhanced my skills in troubleshooting software and hardware problems. I feel these skills would allow me to perform effectively in this position. My enclosed resume outlines my experience in greater detail.

I welcome the opportunity to meet with you and appreciate your consideration. Should you need additional information, you may reach me at (812) 555-7777.

I hope to speak with you soon.

Sincerely,

Chris Austen

##Enclosure

A Sample Cover Letter in Full Block layout

Notice the clean margins on the left side that look pleasing to the eye. Also look how the language veers between a mild formal and conversational tone. The words are neither too slavish nor arrogant in tone. This is what you should be careful about while writing a cover letter. You are expected not to:

    a. Mention your financial issues.
    b. Mention about your hobbies or interests, but do so only in your CV or resume that follows.
    c. Speak ill about your present or past employer.
    d. Mention your expected salary.
    e. Brag about your accomplishments.

Self-Assessment Questions

1. While writing in the modified block layout, everything is aligned towards the left. The remark is:

    i. True
    ii. False
    iii. There is nothing like a modified block layout
    iv. Partly true

2. What should necessarily accompany a CV or a resume?

    i. A bright, nice envelope
    ii. A cover letter
    iii. Your photograph
    iv. All

3. Which of the following is a letter writing layout?

    i. Full Block Layout
    ii. Quarto layout
    iii. Folio layout
    iv. None

4. What should be avoided while writing a cover letter?

    i. Your financial issues

ii. A brief description of your achievements, though not bragging about the same

iii. Your expectations from the company in a line or two

iv. All

5. We still write letters and mail them in the traditional way: this act of sending communication is called:

i. Snail mail

ii. Tortoise mail

iii. Old mail

iv. Victorian mail

F. **Types of External Documents**

You saw the importance of written documentation in the formal scenario. You must have gathered a fair idea by now that despite it being the age of digitisation, written documents still hold their sway, and are a welcome part of any organisational communication setup. In this section, we'll have a look at some of the types of documents that are sent externally. As mentioned, CVs and resumes are also instances of 'external' communication.

1. Order, complaint, appreciation, recommendation letters

a. **An order letter:**

An order letter is sent between two conglomerates or organisations when there is a possibility of exchanging goods or utilities. It should be preferably written within a page and be crisp, and to the point. Any superfluous information is not welcome here:

Sample Order Letter
Manny Manufacturing, Inc.
4378 E. # 4th Street Place, Zip Code
February 5th, 2008 XYZ, Inc
Place,
Zip Code
Attention: Sales Department

I'd like to order (mention the orders in a table). The reference numbers are from your 2003 catalogue. Please include a catalogue with my order.

I want this order to ship COD complete. If you cannot send the complete order within 10 days, please inform me immediately. I can be contacted at 87609967.

Thank you

Name Designation

b. A complaint letter:

As mentioned before, a complaint letter is a document expressing dissatisfaction over the receipt of goods and utilities. It gives an honest opinion of the scenario and should be worded cautiously as any harsh words can sever the erstwhile good ties between the corresponding parties:

Date...

Supplier Name... Company name... Address...

Sub: Complaint Letter for Poor Quality of Materials and replacement of products

Dear (Name),

This is to inform you that the stores deliver by you in our warehouse last week against our supply order dated (date) has been inspected by our quality assurance team under the supervision of the inspector. Feeling sorry to mention here that the entire store supplied by you has been rejected by the quality assurance team and they have endorsed on the delivery challan to return the store back and replace it with the quality store as per specifications and standards of the contract agreement. Keeping above in view you are hereby instructed to replace all the supplied items with quality goods so the agreement is completed in its true letter and spirit.

Hopefully, you will carry out the task as directed as soon as possible to avoid any inconvenience in the later stage, please.

Sincerely Yours, Your name...

Contact no. and signature...

[**Adapted from**: Assignment Point]

c. An appreciation letter:

Appreciation letters are written to appreciate good conduct or the timely delivery of goods and services between two organisations. Suppose company X sent some of its employees for a workshop to company Z to add skills to its task force. If the employees were well received, X is expected to write an appreciation letter to Z, acknowledging its hospitality. It may also look like this:

Avery Jones

123 Main Street, Anytown,

CA 12345 · 555-555-5555 ·

avery.jones@email.com

July 21, 2021

Viola Lee

Vice President, Customer Relations ACME Financial

123 Business Rd. Business City,

NY 54321

Dear Ms. Lee,

Thank you for taking the time to talk with me today. I sincerely appreciate the time you spent reviewing my career goals and recommending strategies for achieving them. Your advice was very helpful and gave me a new perspective on available opportunities.

I especially appreciate your offer to connect me to others in your network. I plan on following up with the contacts you emailed me right away. I will also use the online networking resources you recommended to further my job search.

Any additional suggestions you may have would be welcome. I'll update you as my search progresses.

Again, thank you so much for your help. I greatly appreciate the assistance you have provided me.

best regards

Avery Jones

[**Adapted from** Balance Careers]

d. **A recommendation letter:**

Such letters are written when an organisation recommends someone for a post. For instance, as mentioned in the preceding sub-unit, an organisation needs some security men and asks a security company to supply detailed report about someone. The latter responds by supplying the information in positive terms. This is a recommendation letter and might look like the one given below, albeit in different situations:

[Your Name] [Street Address] [City, St Zip]

[Optional - Email Address] [Today's Date]

[Name of Recipient] [Title]

[Company] [Address] [City, St Zip]

Dear [Name of Recipient]:

[Short introduction paragraph - include a brief statement about who you are and the purpose of the letter]

[Provide details and facts about your relationship to the person being recommended as well as facts about the individual including positions, employment dates and responsibilities.]

[Provide a statement about whether or not the individual is qualified or recommended by you.]

[Provide examples that support your recommendation.]

[Close the letter by summarising your recommendation and stating whether you

would be willing to further communicate with the recipient.] [See Vertex42.com for tips and a sample letter.]

Sincerely (or Respectfully Yours)

(Sign here for letters sent by mail or fax) [Typed Name]

[Title - if applicable]

Self-Assessment Questions

6. You've received a consignment in a bad condition. You're supposed to write:

  i.   A cover letter
  ii. A complaint letter
  iii. An appreciation letter
  iv. A recommendation letter

7. You want to send an employee to some other company for a year and two. You write:

  i.   A cover letter
  ii. A complaint letter
  iii. An appreciation letter
  iv. A recommendation letter

8. You received a good response from a company to whom you'd sent some employees for training. You write:

   i. A cover letter
   ii. A complaint letter
   iii. An appreciation letter
   iv. A recommendation letter

9. Any official letter should preferably be not more than page/s long:

   i. 1 page
   ii. 2 pages
   iii. 3 pages
   iv. 1.5 pages

10. Which of the following is not an example of an 'external' communication?

   i. A cover letter
   ii. A complaint letter
   iii. An appreciation letter
   iv. Minutes of a meeting

G. CVs and resumes

What was called a "bio-data" is now better known as a CV. The term CV stands for "curriculum vitae", a Latin word that means the course of one's life. CVs can run up to many pages if they are detailed in nature. For example, a university professor's CV may run to numerous pages keeping in mind his/her educational qualifications, publications and so forth. On the other hand, a resume is not more than one and a half pages long and is more preferred in corporate settings. The word "resume" is French and it means a "summary", thereby highlighting its brevity.

The heart of the matter is: how to write an effective CV or resume? Of course, you have ready- made CV or resume builders like zety.com and other allied sites that help you design an effective document.

A CV, which stands for curriculum vitae, is a document used when applying for jobs. It allows you to summarise your education, skills and experience enabling you to successfully sell your abilities to potential employers. Alongside your CV employers also usually ask for a cover letter.

In the USA and Canada CVs are known as résumés. These documents tend to be more concise and follow no particular formatting rules.

It is advisable to include these things with your CV or resume:

    a. Your profile along with a photograph, if possible
    b. Your educational qualifications
    c. Your work experience
    d. Skills and achievements
    e. References

As mentioned before, a cover letter should accompany your CV or resume. If you are emailing the employer, do write your cover letter in the body of the email and include your CV or resume as an attachment.

Summary

Official communication can be either external or internal in nature. By external, we mean that there is room for external communication within the formal communicative scenario, and by internal we imply that the same communicative strategy can happen within the organisation.

Emails are still considered the most efficient and inexpensive way to send messages. Emails were possible due the development of the first internet services in the 1990s. The ARPANET was the first digital messaging service linking select institutions in the USA in the 1970s.

Internal communication can be upward, downward, diagonal or grapevine in nature. The last communication is unofficial in nature, while the others are usually considered official.

Email correspondences should have proper subject lines along with adherence to the register and communicative event.

Terminal Questions

1. What is meant by internal communication? List some of its features.

1. What is meant by upward communication? How does it differ f rom grapevine communication? Provide some examples.

3. Give a brief history of email and the Internet.

4 What are the steps to be followed in email writing?

Activity

Activity type: Offline Duration: 40 Minutes

Description:

Mr. T has to email a difficult client. The conversation will surround the intention of the legal firm for which Mr. T works to provide legal advice to the client as to how to repay old debts without involving any problems to a third party that has been harassing the client. The latter is 'difficult' to handle as he is prone to fits of anger and any imbalance here may trigger issues for both the client as well as the legal firm that are partners.

Now answer the questions:

a.   What points should Mr. T keep in mind before emailing his client?

b.   From this brief case study, do you think proper email etiquette is a must, at least in formal settings?

c.   Do you think Mr. T should use a proof-reading app/tool like Grammarly to communicate better?

End Notes

1. *Forbes.* "15 ways you can improve internal communication." https://www.forbes.com/sites/forbesagencycouncil/2017/11/08/ending-confusion-
15-ways-you-can-improve-internal-communications/?sh=2bc226c344f0. Accessed 15 Sep 2024.

2. ---. "Go write a letter." https://www.forbes.com/sites/theyec/2020/05/06/go-write-a-letter-ink-and-paper-inthe-
digital-age/?sh=65c3d1aa46e1. Accessed 12 Dec 2024.

3. Michael Page. "What is a Cover Letter and Why They Are Important?" https://www.michaelpage.co.uk/advice/career-advice/cover-letter-and-cv-advice/
why-cover-letters-are-
important#:~:text=A%20cover%20letter%20accompanies%20
your,why%20you%20want%20the%20position. Accessed 15 June 2024.

BIBLIOGRAPHY

External Resources

Chan, J. M. (2005). *E-mail: A Write it Well Guide*. Write It Well Books.

Gattiker, U. E. (1990). *Organisations & Communications Technology*. Sage Publications. 1st volume of Contemporary Communication Research.

Roche, M. (2019). *Business Emails*. IDM Business English Books.

Rogers, E. M., *et al.* (1976). *Communication in Organisations*. Free Press.

Video links

Topic

Link

Internal communication

https://www.youtube.com/watch?v=dLF5b3qp6hg

External communication

https://www.youtube.com/watch?v=7UNna3tf160

https://www.youtube.com/watch?v=jj0oSr89mog

Direction of

communication

https://www.youtube.com/watch?v=5LirDjpRupU

E-mail etiquette

https://www.youtube.com/watch?v=oI3rVQFye9w

https://www.youtube.com/watch?v=c8yvN5oOKHY

Select Bibliography

Alexander, L. G. (2000). *Longman English Grammar Practice*. Longman.

Azar, B. S. (2003). *Understanding and Using English Grammar*. Pearson Education.

Biber, D., Conrad, S., & Leech, G. (2002). *Longman Grammar of Spoken and Written English*. Longman.

Brown, H. D. (2007). *Principles of Language Learning and Teaching*. Pearson Education.

Byrne, D. (1991). *Teaching Writing Skills*. Longman.

Canale, M., & Swain, M. (1980). *Theoretical Bases of Communicative Approaches to Second Language Teaching and Testing*. Applied Linguistics, 1(1), 1-47.

Carter, R., & McCarthy, M. (2006). *Cambridge Grammar of English*. Cambridge University Press.

Celce-Murcia, M. (2001). *Teaching English as a Second or Foreign Language*. Heinle & Heinle.

Chomsky, N. (1957). *Syntactic Structures*. Mouton.

Crystal, D. (2003). *English as a Global Language*. Cambridge University Press.

Day, R. R., & Bamford, J. (1998). *Top Ten Principles for Teaching ESL/ EFL Writing*. ESL Writing, 1(1), 16-28.

Ellis, R. (2006). *The Study of Second Language Acquisition*. Oxford University Press.

Ellis, R. (2003). *Task-Based Language Learning and Teaching*. Oxford University Press.

Fraser, B. (2010). *Pragmatic Competence:* The Case of Hedging. Routledge.

Goh, C. C. M., & Burns, A. (2012). *Teaching Speaking: A Holistic Approach*. Cambridge University Press.

Greenbaum, S., & Quirk, R. (1990). *A Student's Grammar of the English Language*. Longman.

Hinkel, E. (2016). *Teaching English Grammar to Speakers of Other Languages*. Routledge.

Hudson, R. (2000). *Essential Introductory Linguistics*. Blackwell.

Halliday, M. A. K. (2004). *An Introduction to Functional Grammar*. Edward Arnold.

Hewings, M. (2005). *Advanced Grammar in Use*. Cambridge University Press.

Hughes, A. (2003). *Testing for Language Teachers*. Cambridge University Press.

James, C. (2013). *Errors in Language Learning and Use: Exploring Error Analysis*. Routledge.

Jones, L. (2011). *Practical English Usage*. Oxford University Press.

Kane, T. S. (2011). *The Oxford Essential Guide to Writing*. Oxford University Press.

Larsen-Freeman, D. (2003). *Teaching and Testing Grammar*. In N. Schmitt (Ed.), An Introduction to Applied Linguistics (pp. 247-263). Routledge.

Leech, G. (2004). *Meaning and the English Verb*. Pearson Education.

Lyle, S. (2008). *Communicative English Grammar*. Cengage Learning.

McCarthy, M., & O'Keeffe, A. (2004). *Vocabulary in Use: Upper-Intermediate*. Cambridge University Press.

McArthur, T. (1992). *The Oxford Companion to the English Language*. Oxford University Press.

Moffett, J. (1968). *Teaching the Universe of Discourse*. Houghton Mifflin.

Murphy, R. (2012). *English Grammar in Use*. Cambridge University Press.

Nunan, D. (1991). *Language Teaching Methodology*. Prentice Hall.

O'Grady, W., Archibald, J., & Katamba, F. (2010). *Contemporary Linguistic Analysis: An Introduction*. Pearson Education.

O'Keeffe, A., McCarthy, M., & Carter, R. (2007). *From Corpus to Classroom: Language Use and Language Teaching*. Cambridge University Press.

Pennington, M. C., & Richards, J. C. (2016). *Second Language Teacher Education*. Routledge.

Phillips, D. (1993). *Longman English Grammar*. Longman.

Quirk, R., Greenbaum, S., Leech, G., & Svartvik, J. (1985). *A Comprehensive Grammar of the English Language*. Longman.

Radford, A. (2009). *An Introduction to English Syntax*. Pearson Education.

Richards, J. C. (2001). *Curriculum Development in Language Teaching*. Cambridge University Press.

Richards, J. C., & Schmidt, R. (2002). *Longman Dictionary of Language Teaching and Applied Linguistics*. Pearson Education.

Robins, R. H. (2002). *General Linguistics: An Introductory Survey.* Routledge.

Schmitt, N. (2010). *Vocabulary in Language Teaching.* Cambridge University Press.

Searle, J. R. (1969). *Speech Acts: An Essay in the Philosophy of Language.* Cambridge University Press.

Thornbury, S. (2005). *How to Teach Speaking.* Pearson Education.

Trask, R. L. (1999). *Key Concepts in Language and Linguistics.* Routledge.

Ur, P. (1996). *A Course in English Language Teaching.* Cambridge University Press.

VanPatten, B., & Williams, J. (2007). *Theories in Second Language Acquisition: Introduction.* Routledge.

Wardhaugh, R. (2006). *An Introduction to Sociolinguistics.* Blackwell.

White, R. (1988). *The ELT Curriculum: Design and Implementation.* Basil Blackwell.

Widdowson, H. G. (1990). *Aspects of Language Teaching.* Oxford University Press.

Yule, G. (2006). *The Study of Language.* Cambridge University Press.

About The Author

Dr. Arnab Chatterjee is a Professor of English at the Centre for Distance and Online Education, Chandigarh University, Mohali, Punjab; India. Prior to this, he was Professor and Head of the Department of Humanities, Budge Budge Institute of Technology, Kolkata (under MAKAUT University) and an Administrative Officer of IQAC. He was also with the CDOE, KL Deemed to be University, Vijayawada; Andhra Pradesh as an Associate Professor and co-coordinator of the KL Global Writing Centre. He has around 10 years of experience in both ODL as well as conventional modes of instruction. He has taught at Netaji Subhas Open University, Indira Gandhi National Open University, Directorate of Distance Education, Rabindra Bharati University; Kolkata and DDE, The University of Burdwan, West Bengal. He is a member of prestigious institutions like the Sahitya Akademi, New Delhi, and the Modern Language Association of America, USA. He is also a prolific poet and has his own Amazon author page. His areas of interest in the ODL/OL mode of instruction include learner satisfaction, the ARCS model, and a peep beyond it. This is his 5th academic book.